Scripture From Scratch II

THE WORLD OF THE BIBLE

Study Guide

Elizabeth McNamer
and
Virginia Smith

ST. ANTHONY MESSENGER PRESS
AND FRANCISCAN COMMUNICATIONS
Cincinnati, Ohio

Nihil Obstat: Rev. Nicholas Lohkamp, O.F.M.
Rev. Edward J. Gratsch
Imprimi Potest: Rev. John Bok, O.F.M., Provincial
Imprimatur: Most Reverend Carl K. Moeddel, V.G.
Archdiocese of Cincinnati
August 26, 1996

The *nihil obstat* and *imprimatur* are a declaration that a book is considered to be free from doctrinal or moral error. It is not implied that those who have granted the *nihil obstat* and *imprimatur* agree with the contents, opinions or statements expressed. Scripture citations are taken from *The New American Bible With Revised New Testament*, copyright ©1986 by the Confraternity of Christian Doctrine, and are used by permission. All rights reserved.

Cover and book design by Julie Lonneman and Sandy Digman

ISBN 0-86716-276-7

Published by St. Anthony Messenger Press
Printed in the U.S.A.

Contents

Contents

Preface

During the early years of the 1980's, I was happily engaged in leading an adult study group in my parish. Having long been convinced that a major share of the Church's educational ministry should be directed toward those members of our congregation generally termed grown-ups, I was having a wonderful time leading my troops down one fascinating avenue after another. We spent some time wandering through the maze of Vatican II documents and then took a side trip through the area of death and dying. Mostly, however, we spent our time cruising the highway I like best (one of the advantages of being a leader is that you get to map out the journey): We traveled many a figurative mile into the world of the Bible.

It was here that our small but very enthusiastic group seemed most at home. Whatever we covered (and we covered everything from the creation accounts to biblical geography), they couldn't seem to get enough. They were obviously enjoying themselves (and their God) hugely, and I couldn't have been happier.

Well, that's not entirely true. I *could* have been happier because what began as an insignificant problem began to assume growing importance—and with that importance came the conviction that something needed to be done about it. The problem did not involve those who were faithfully attending every session regardless of the wind, the rain or the dinner dishes in the sink. It involved those who *weren't* attending.

Now, I'm not so naive as to expect that half the parish is going to turn out for any given project—or a fourth of the parish or even a tenth. Much as one might like them to, it's simply not realistic.

The "bother" came from those who would approach me almost furtively and ask a question about something biblical. Others would slyly suggest that I give a talk on some special aspect of the Bible. Some of these behind-the-hand queries had the air of conspiracy about them, as though the questioner were afraid of being overheard and thereby thoroughly embarrassed. Each time I would invite the person to come to the sessions already in progress, only to have them recoil as if invited to an IRS audit. When I asked why the prospect seemed so distasteful, the reply generally had something to do with the fact that the established weekly get-together was much too advanced. I would tactfully try to point out that a person who had never attended a session was at a singular disadvantage in making such a judgment, but to no avail. Interested they might be, but they simply refused to step over the threshold and into what might loosely be termed a class.

As time went on and this strange phenomenon continued to occur, I grew increasingly concerned that there were numbers—possibly *large* numbers—of people who sincerely wanted to start down the road to meet God in the word, but evidently they weren't about to take any established route. How could they be drawn in on a path that seemed easy and natural for them?

Conversations with a variety of parishioners, some active in Bible studies and some not, brought to the surface what was to me a rather surprising deduction: Many, if not most, adult Catholics suffer from what can only be termed an inferiority complex when it comes to the Bible. They sense that their knowledge is inadequate (which may be true) and that this inadequacy is somehow their fault (which decidedly is not true). Further probing turned up the not-at-all surprising corollary that, feeling the way they do, people in this predicament are not about to expose themselves to any situation in which this supposedly culpable flaw would be likely to surface. Hence, their reticence to become part of group projects. However inclined they might be to go it alone and try to remedy their lack of biblical education in the privacy of their own homes, most are unable to do so, since they do not know where to look for resources or how to use them.

Clearly, this was a catch-22 situation. The remedy seemed to lie in coaxing potential Bible-lovers from behind their drawn drapes and back into the mainstream where they would overcome their inferiority complex through the discovery that, far from being the lone parishioner in this predicament, they were probably in the majority.

How could these wary souls be cajoled into appearing at a public gathering? Well, maybe if they wouldn't come to an ongoing series for six or eight or ten weeks, possibly they'd take a chance on a single afternoon. Nothing too horrifying could occur in four short hours, especially if there was no requirement on their part to open their mouths.

High on the list of priorities would have to be a sincere attempt not to send people scurrying back to their drawn drapes by presenting material which was beyond them or which was loaded with such jargon as *exegesis*, *hermeneutics*, *eschatology*. Equally important would be the presentation of modern Catholic Scripture scholarship in a manner befitting the intelligence of modern Catholic adults: a solid meat-and-potatoes message, not one composed of little more than fluff and whipped cream.

It would be a given that *no* previous Bible study would be required or even expected. And certainly there should be plenty of open spaces for socializing over coffee and cookies while chatting about the content of the presentations, the content of the morning paper or the rules of the latest diet fad, whatever came to mind.

All in all, it seemed to come down to delivering basic Bible in a highly digestible manner, starting from square one—starting from scratch. At this point, I knew I would need more (and possibly better) input than my own, so I contacted longtime friend and fellow Scripture student Elizabeth McNamer and asked if she'd be willing to take a little time from her already packed schedule to try this experimental venture. After all, it would only be for one afternoon, and we would only issue invitations to her parish and mine. Happily, she agreed to throw her lot in with me (only for one afternoon), and we set about publicizing our upcoming enterprise.

Weeks of painstaking preparation culminated on a Sunday in November as *Scripture From Scratch* was launched in possibly the worst snowstorm in years. Just as we were consoling ourselves with the thought that it would probably be good for us to do the program once simply for ourselves, folks began arriving—and arriving and arriving. The final count was something over ninety.

At the close of the day, enthusiasts were asking when the next session was scheduled and what it would contain. We managed neatly to sidestep that issue, giving no indication that a second session had not even been envisioned, much less planned.

But plan we did, and soon a second *Scripture From Scratch* presentation sprang into being, only to be followed in rapid succession by sessions three and four. It was becoming apparent that presentations could be added indefinitely but, having provided overviews of most parts of the Bible, we elected to stop there. We concluded (rightly as it turned out) that these four presentations would keep us as busy as we wanted to be. (Both of us had other teaching positions which required us to turn up in our respective classrooms on a more or less regular basis.)

We needed to remind ourselves, too, that *Scripture From Scratch* was not intended to be a full-blown study program. Rather, its primary purpose was to get adult Catholics over that initial reserve. The object was to bring them to the point where, after attending one or more *Scripture From Scratch* sessions, they at long last felt comfortable enough and interested enough and enthusiastic enough to continue studying Scripture.

Out-of-towners present for the pilot session apparently spread the word when they arrived home. Invitations began to arrive from around the diocese, then from around the rest of Montana, then from out of state. Without much concerted effort on our part, the program was assuming a life of its own. How did God want to use this program (and us who came with the package)? Did the project have any worth at all in the divine scheme of things? We hoped that Gamaliel's comments to the Sanhedrin regarding the preaching of the apostles would in some sense apply to *Scripture From Scratch*: "For if this endeavor or this activity is of human origin, it will destroy itself. But if it comes from God, you will not be able to destroy [it]" (Acts 5:38b-39a).

Now an unprecedented opportunity makes *Scripture From Scratch* available to more persons, parishes and places than would ever be possible for us in person. The wonderful world of videotapes and the warm support of the St. Anthony Messenger Press staff have allowed us to place what we hope will be a useful tool in many hands. Our prayerful good wishes are with you as you begin the glorious discovery that exploring the magnificent word of God can (and should) be fascinating, nonthreatening, exhilarating, enlightening, habit-forming and even fun.

Virginia Smith
1991

Reflections Five Years Later

Rereading words written five years ago, I find that most remain valid, but more needs to be said. At one point in my initial remarks, I commented that soon after its inception, *Scripture From Scratch* seemed to assume a life of its own. It wasn't so much that Elizabeth and I planned and executed the next step in the program's development. Rather, it seemed to take off into uncharted waters, dragging us in its wake. This situation has, if anything, intensified with the passing of time.

The response to the original *Scripture From Scratch* videos has been extremely gratifying. Elizabeth and I would have been delighted with any evidence that the program was proving helpful to a person or two here, a parish or two there. Publishers are often not quite so easily pleased, so our thanks go to all who helped make our program sufficiently successful to spawn a spin-off, *Scripture From Scratch* in print. If you haven't yet encountered this four-page monthly guide to understanding the Bible, you're about to, since references to particular issues are liberally sprinkled throughout this study manual. We are especially pleased that so many notable names in biblical studies have contributed to its pages. We hope that you will find each issue informational and intriguing.

Now a second set of videos, *Scripture From Scratch II: The World of the Bible*, joins the original set, *Scripture From Scratch: A Basic Bible Study Program*. As we indicated in the introduction to the facilitator's manual for the original videos, our intent was never to make *Scripture From Scratch* a comprehensive program, but rather to meet the needs of those who simply wanted to learn the basics of Bible study. To that end, we felt that placing the books of the Bible in context with their time, place and situation would prove helpful.

The eight video programs of *Scripture From Scratch II: The World of the Bible* deal with the world of the Hebrew and Christian Scriptures— its geography, history and archaeology; the religious concepts of the Hebrew people; the religious life and political climate of Jesus' day;

the historical Jesus. Perhaps these videos will make a world of difference in your enjoyment of and benefit from those amazing writings that make up the Bible.

Virginia Smith
1996

Introduction

Scripture From Scratch is an experience of God's word for all Catholic adults. Two videos and a publication with the same name are designed for those who want to know more about the Bible but don't know where to begin. No previous Bible study is required, though *Scripture From Scratch* will benefit those who have already had some experience with the Bible.

The first video series, *Scripture From Scratch: A Basic Bible Study Program*, gives a general introduction to Scripture and an overview of the Bible, the Old Testament, the New Testament and the Gospels in sixteen one-hour programs.

This second video series, *Scripture From Scratch II: The World of the Bible*, fills in the background to the writings. Programs One through Four deal with the Old Testament: the geography of the biblical lands, words and religious concepts found in the Old Testament, a brief history of the Hebrew people and the archaeology of the Bible. Programs Five through Eight elucidate the New Testament: the religious climate in Palestine at the time of Jesus, the political situation in the first century of the common era, everyday life and Jesus in his own historical context. Each video program lasts about twenty-five minutes and is filled to the brim with basic information about the Bible presented in a clear, easy-to-follow, nonthreatening manner.

Faithful use of the study manual will help you to absorb and remember the abundance of material in *Scripture From Scratch II*. For each video program we have provided a Session Outline with space for your own notes and a Review section. After you have watched the video, take ten minutes to look at the Buzzwords and then write a brief summary of what you have learned.

The sections designated For Discussion suggest that you jot down any questions you have for sharing in small groups of three or four people. This section also provides other topics for your small-group discussion. Your group may then share its conclusions with the entire group of *Scripture From Scratch* participants. In addition, the study manual suggests Follow-Up Activities you can carry out alone between sessions.

All of the study manual's components are designed to reinforce what you have learned after viewing each video program. Writing down what you have learned within twenty minutes of hearing it will help you retain the information better. Small groups give each person an opportunity to voice his or her concerns. Large groups help solidify and make clear the subject under discussion. The weekly activities will keep your interest long after viewing the videos and participating in discussions and activities.

You will need a Bible. A biblical commentary or other resource material may also prove helpful. At the end of this manual you will find a bibliography containing annotated lists of Bible translations and other resource materials, as well as a reading list for further study of particular topics. All of these books should be available from your local libraries or through inter-library loan.

Facilitators of *Scripture From Scratch II: The World of the Bible* will want to consult the appendix, which contain practical, nuts-and-bolts information for leading a group and a description of the facilitator's job.

A valuable resource for this and any Bible study program is the monthly publication *Scripture From Scratch* (also from St. Anthony Messenger Press), which deals with a variety of biblical topics. You can subscribe to this publication or order back issues by calling, toll-free, 1-800-488-0488.

Virginia Smith and I hope that viewing and discussing *Scripture From Scratch II: The World of the Bible* will not only excite but also encourage you to dig deeper into God's word and thereby be immensely enriched.

Elizabeth McNamer
1996

The Catholic Approach to Scripture Study

At some point, you may have been on the receiving end of a question like this: "Why doesn't the Catholic Church want its members to read the Bible?" Or this: "Why isn't the Catholic Church a Bible-centered Church?" While these questions and others like them are far from rare in our pluralistic society, many of us tend to fumble and mumble a lot when faced with them.

What *does* the Catholic Church see as the Bible's rightful place in theology and practice? Are Catholics encouraged to read, study and pray with the Bible? Is there a Catholic approach to Scripture study? If so, what is it?

The fact that these issues come to the fore so often should tell us something about the attitude of post-Vatican II Catholics toward the Bible. In the years since the Second Vatican Council convened in 1962, interest in matters scriptural has grown by leaps and bounds in Catholic lay circles. Catholics are actively seeking Bible study groups that offer leadership in understanding God's word. Unfortunately, many Catholics perceive little or no difference among these study groups. After all, if they have as their central purpose an earnest desire to learn more about the books of the Old and New Testaments, how different can they be? As it turns out, these study groups can be very different indeed.

To find out how the Church in our own time looks at the Bible, we need to drop back a few decades to a time when Pope Pius XII was at the helm of Peter's boat, steering it through the tumultuous seas created by World War II. Nearly every nation on earth was involved in this global conflict either directly or indirectly, and so was almost every individual. The focal point of every circumstance was its impact on the war effort. In a very real sense, the entire planet was under attack.

Little wonder, then, that a papal encyclical from the pen of Pius XII, one that would later be acknowledged as one of his greatest, failed to receive proper appreciation when first promulgated. An encyclical is simply a letter intended for general circulation, and this particular message to the universal Church, titled *Divino afflante Spiritu*, plunged Catholicism into the modern age of Scripture scholarship and research. Following centuries of seeing Saint Jerome's Vulgate (Latin) version of the Scriptures as the starting point for all biblical investigation, researchers were now free, even encouraged, to bypass Jerome's fifth-century work in favor of the much older Hebrew, Aramaic and Greek manuscripts. (Although no original manuscript exists for any biblical book, Old Testament or New, texts of these books do exist in their original languages.)

Not only did Pius XII open avenues of opportunity to translators, but he also swung open the door leading to a variety of areas in biblical study, stating categorically that a genuine understanding of the biblical books was impossible without considering the time period and culture from which they sprang, the type of literature the writer used, the audience for whom the books were originally intended and the author's intent in selecting particular themes.

As soon as World War II ended and world conditions became somewhat stabilized, modern Catholic biblical study began in earnest. The 1960's brought the twentieth century's landmark event for Catholics. Pope John XXIII changed the face of the Church forever by convening the Second Vatican Council. The world's bishops met to reexamine the very essence of the Church, restating long-held doctrines and dogmas in ways more suitable for a postwar world that was continuing to change at a pace unparalleled in human history.

Between 1962 and 1965, sixteen documents emerged from this council. Each would impact Catholic thought and practice, some more obviously than others. To this day, many Catholics view Vatican II primarily as the source of earthshaking changes in liturgical practice. Most of these were set down in the *Constitution on the Sacred Liturgy*.

Of equal importance in the eyes of Scripture enthusiasts was the *Dogmatic Constitution on Divine Revelation* (*Dei verbum*), which underscored Pius XII's earlier teaching and expanded it even further. Regarding the use of the Bible for prayer and study by all Catholics and the availability of modern translations, the document reads:

Access to sacred Scripture ought to be open wide to the Christian faithful. For this reason the Church, from the very beginning, made her own the ancient translation of the Old Testament called the Septuagint; she honors also the other Eastern translations, and the Latin translations, especially that which is called the Vulgate. But since the Word of God must be readily available to all times, the Church, with motherly concern, sees to it that suitable and correct translations are made into various languages.... (#22)

Again emphasizing the approach to Scripture outlined in *Divino afflante Spiritu*, the Council fathers said:

Seeing that, in sacred Scripture, God speaks through people in human fashion, it follows that the interpreter of sacred Scriptures, to ascertain what God has wished to communicate to us, should carefully search out the meaning the sacred writers really had in mind, that meaning which God had thought well to manifest through the medium of their words.

In determining the intention of the sacred writers, attention must be paid, *inter alia*, to "literary forms for the fact is that truth is differently presented and expressed in the various types of historical writing, in prophetical and poetical texts" and in other forms of literary expression. Hence the exegete must look for that meaning which the sacred writer, in a determined situation and given the circumstances of his time and culture, intended to express and did in fact express, through the medium of a contemporary literary form. Rightly to understand what the sacred author wanted to affirm in his work, due attention must be paid both to the customary and characteristic patterns of perception, speech and narrative which prevailed at the age of the sacred writer, and to the conventions which the people of his time followed in their dealings with one another. (#12)

One more citation from *Dei verbum* helps the essentials of the Catholic approach to Scripture truly to emerge:

In order that the full and living Gospel might always be preserved in the Church the apostles left bishops as their successors. They gave them "their own position of teaching authority." This sacred Tradition, then, and the sacred Scripture of both Testaments, are like a mirror in which the Church, during its pilgrim journey here on earth, contemplates God, from whom it receives everything, until such time as it is brought to see him face to face as he really is.... Sacred Tradition and sacred Scripture, then, are bound closely together and communicate one with the other.... Sacred Tradition and sacred Scripture make up a single sacred deposit of the Word of God, which is entrusted to the Church. (#7, 9, 10)

This sampling of the Council document provides several insights into the mind of the Church today respecting the Bible:

1) The Bible is intended to be available to all the faithful.

2) Translations should be invitingly readable and constantly updated as more and newer data become accessible.

3) Understanding of biblical writings *must* take into consideration the times and circumstances in which they were composed plus such related factors as their literary style, the sources utilized, the culture and the audience originally intended.

4) For Catholics, the Bible does not stand as the sole source of divine revelation. The Church stands today, as it consistently has, on the twin pillars of Scripture and Tradition, seeing in each the reflection of the other.

Historical Criticism

Motivated by the strong support of popes and bishops, Catholic Scripture experts moved rapidly to put the Church in the forefront of contemporary Bible research. Today Catholicism can take its proper place among other Christian traditions in the various areas of biblical endeavor.

The umbrella approach that gained great favor among Catholic scholars as well as those from a number of mainline Protestant denominations came to be called *historical criticism*. But for many average Catholics getting their first taste of Scripture scholarship, the word *criticism* is a stumbling block. Tending to associate the word more with fault-finding than with examination, some back away from what seems to them an exercise in picking the Bible to pieces. In reality, the historical-critical method seeks to do what both Pope Pius XII and Vatican II recommended: analyze and evaluate the sacred books from as many angles as possible in order to extract every potential nuance of meaning. Historical criticism, then, is correctly viewed as a detailed investigation. To assess it as a hostile attempt at correction is to miss its meaning entirely.

The post-Vatican II Bible "boom" among scholars has more than been matched by the enthusiasm of the Catholic in the pew. Interest in Bible studies has mushroomed in recent decades, and interest shows no sign of abating soon. On the contrary, the thirst for biblical knowledge seems far from being slaked, and the Church's Scripture pros are doing an admirable job of providing a continuing stream of commentaries, dictionaries, concordances, atlases, magazines and books on any and all matters biblical. A rather limited listing of some of these may be found in the Bibliography (see page 77).

Sadly, the majority of these works were not yet available when the initial force of biblical fervor burst upon the Church immediately following Vatican II. In truth, no one (with the possible exception of the Holy Spirit) could have envisioned such a passionate pursuit among people who hadn't exactly gained a reputation as avid Bible readers in the past. Solid, reputable materials were assembled as fast as possible, but not fast enough for some. Under the sincere but often erroneous assumption that a Bible study is a Bible study is a Bible study, large numbers of Catholics joined groups whose basic approach to the sacred books was fundamentalist—very far from that taken by the Church.

Again it should be stressed that the Catholic manner of viewing the Bible today is shared by a number of mainline Protestant traditions. This is one situation in which *Scripture From Scratch* attempts to lend a hand. It is our aim to present the Catholic conception of the Bible in every presentation we make. In the process, we assume we will be welcomed among Christians of other denominational traditions as well. Scripture professionals from many backgrounds are working together in this ecumenical age. Much of the unraveling of our common thread is past, thankfully, but interested parties on all sides agree that nothing is gained by ignoring honest differences or failing to address them. Such differences are real and must be acknowledged. It is therefore essential that every attempt be made to honor those beliefs which are strongly held by others while holding to our hearts those which are dear to us, all the while trusting that the Holy Spirit will in time overcome our divisions.

On the Road Again: Geography in the Hebrew Scriptures

Presented by Virginia Smith

Program Outline

Geography has a direct bearing on a people's culture, history, development and language. Understanding biblical incidents is difficult without some knowledge of their locale.

Nearly all events recorded in the Hebrew Scriptures took place in or around the Fertile Crescent, an area that arched from Mesopotamia, the land between the Tigris and Euphrates Rivers in the east, to Egypt in the west. Sumeria, one of the earliest urban societies on earth (c. 3500 B.C.E.), grew up at the eastern end of the Fertile Crescent as the biblical period began and is counterbalanced by Egypt, an incredible civilization nearly as old, at the western tip.

On the eastern shore of the Mediterranean Sea lay Canaan, a narrow strip linking Mesopotamia to Egypt. These lands were already ancient when biblical history began.

Patriarchal Period

Abraham, usually considered the first historical figure in the Hebrew Scriptures, made the first of many biblical journeys around the Fertile Crescent when called by God to undertake a mysterious odyssey to an unspecified destination (Genesis 12:1-3). His arrival in Canaan provided a focal point for biblical history and brought God's people, at least metaphorically, to the Promised Land (at various points, called Canaan, Palestine, Israel, the Holy Land, Judea). This land was promised to Abraham by God (Genesis 15:7), and it is impossible to overstate its importance.

Abraham's son Isaac and grandson Jacob (Israel) continued to live in the area of Canaan. Both retraced Abraham's steps back around the Fertile Crescent, seeking wives from among their own people.

Regional famine took Jacob's sons to Egypt, where they remained for some four centuries, originally living well but ultimately reduced to slavery.

Exodus

The Exodus (departure) from Egypt was led by Moses. Some of this geography is provided in the Book of Exodus, much is not. Although routes through the Sinai Desert are inconclusive and the forty-year time frame may not be literal, the years of the Exodus experience may be the most decisive in Israelite history, ending with the conquest of Canaan under the leadership of Joshua.

Settling Into Canaan

Joshua distributed the land among all the tribes except Levi, which was set aside for the service of God. The Philistine presence along the Mediterranean coast precluded Israelite seaports. Some two hundred years, called the Period of the Judges, followed settlement of the land and demonstrated that knowledge of geography involved a great deal more than being able to locate specific sites. Understanding climatic and soil conditions was equally important, and during this era the Israelites gradually learned how to scratch a living from the land given them.

Israel Under the Monarchy

When the tribes united under a single king, Saul (c. 1020 B.C.E.), the political state of Israel was formally created. The land area was basically the same as that allotted by Joshua. Under Saul's successor, David, those boundaries were greatly expanded. Jerusalem was finally taken and became the nation's capital. Israel's holdings were extended even farther under David's son, Solomon.

Israel and Judah

The united kingdom came to an end during the reign of Solomon's son, Rehoboam, when ten tribes seceded to form the northern kingdom of Israel, leaving the tribes of Benjamin and Judah to become a separate state bearing Judah's name. In 721 B.C.E., the mighty Assyrian Empire swept down on Israel, deporting great numbers of its people and ending its formal existence. Judah, in turn, fell victim in 587 B.C.E. to the superpower of its day, Babylonia. Its captive people trekked back around the Fertile Crescent to Babylon.

Exile

The half-century exile to Babylon was the lowest point in Hebrew history, and the name of this city would ever after conjure up unpleasant associations, much as the name *Auschwitz* does today.

Restoration

When the exile ended in 538 B.C.E., the Jewish remnant traveled back around the Fertile Crescent to try to restore the ruined land and the devastated Jerusalem. Some Jews remained in Babylon; others settled outside the Promised Land in areas such as Egypt. This dispersion was known as the Diaspora.

Foreign influence shifted to the northwest. Alexander the Great spearheaded Greek conquest in the fourth century B.C.E. Pompey took Jerusalem in 63 B.C.E., so the final years of the Hebrew Scriptures found Judah (latinized to Judea) incorporated into the powerful Roman Empire. The stage was set for an amazing event soon to take place in a small Judean village called Bethlehem.

Your Notes

Review

See if you can define the following:

Fertile Crescent

Mesopotamia

Sumeria

Ziggurat

Cuneiform

Ur

Haran

Goshen

Canaan

Assyria

Babylonia

Judah/Judea

Summing Up

Take five minutes to sum up what you have learned.

For Discussion

Your Questions

In the space below, write any questions you have. Share these questions in your small group. After your small group's discussion, report its conclusions to the larger group.

Other Possible
Topics for
Discussion

- How geography influences theology in the Hebrew Scriptures

- How geography influences theology today

- Ways in which geographical locations or traits become metaphors for broader ideas (Babylon, Armageddon, Mecca, Jordan River and so on)

Follow-Up Activities

On Your Own

Trace the religious development of the area in which you live to see what, if any, role geography played in it.

For Further Reading

Scripture From Scratch[1]:

Smith, Virginia. "Exodus and Exile: Shaping God's People." N0295

_____. "Mapping the Biblical Journey." N0694

Catholic Update:

Scott, Macrina, O.S.F. "A Popular Guide to Reading the Bible." C1284

Smith, Virginia. "The Whole Bible at a Glance—Its 'Golden Thread' of Meaning." C0489

---

[1]*Scripture From Scratch* and *Catholic Update* are inexpensive, four-page handouts published by St. Anthony Messenger Press, 1615 Republic Street, Cincinnati, OH 45210.

Map

The Biblical World

The arrows indicate
the route of Abraham.

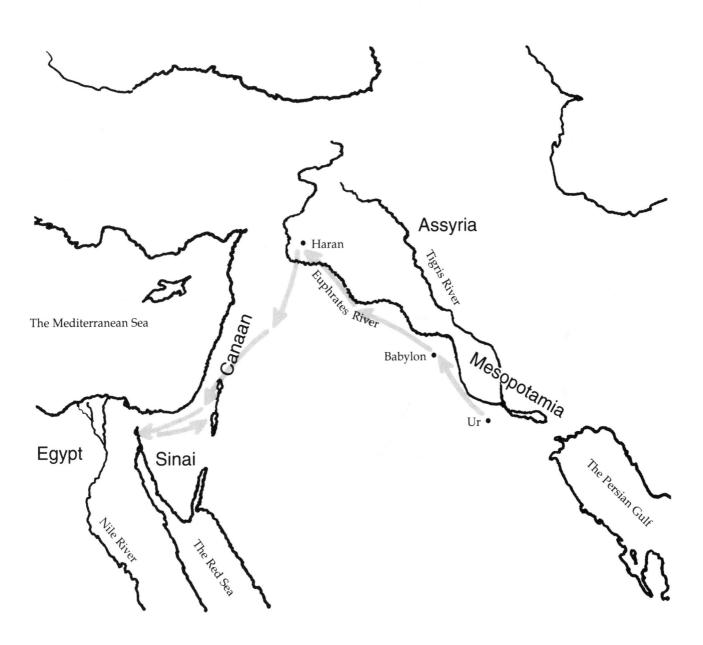

Assyria

• Haran

Tigris River

Euphrates River

The Mediterranean Sea

Canaan

Babylon •

Mesopotamia

Egypt

Sinai

Ur •

The Persian Gulf

Nile River

The Red Sea

Map

The Exodus

The arrows indicate
the route of the Exodus.

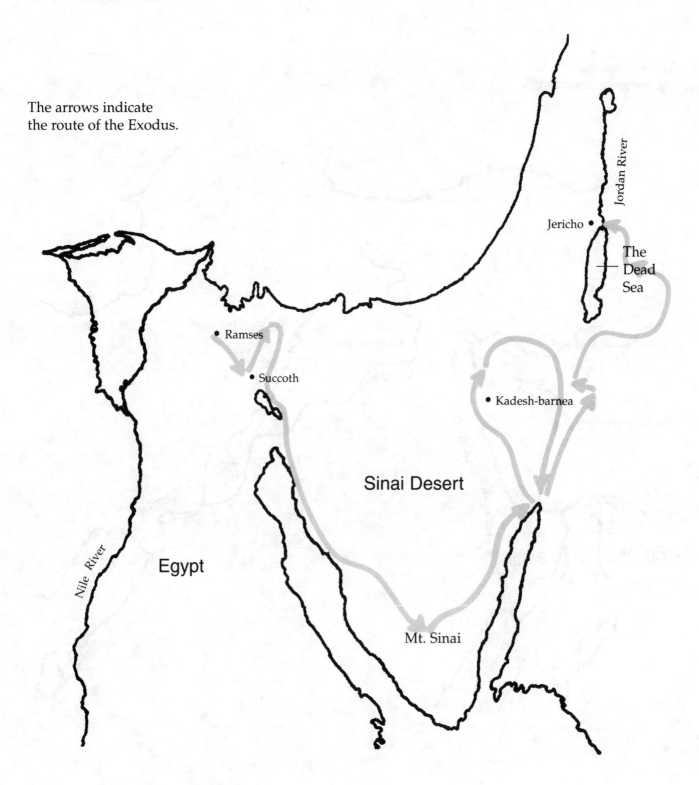

Map

The Kingdoms of Israel and Judah

Phoenicia

The Mediterranean Sea

Sea of Chinnereth
(Sea of Galilee)

• Jezreel

ISRAEL

• Samaria

Jordan River

• Shiloh

Jericho •

• Jerusalem

Philistia

Judah

Dead Sea

Moab

• Beer-sheba

The Vocabulary of Faith: Religious Concepts in the Hebrew Scriptures

Presented by Elizabeth McNamer

Program Outline

We focus now on some key religious concepts of the Hebrew people: God, covenant, circumcision, the Law, the Ark of the Covenant, shrines, priests, prophets, kings, sacrifice, altars, the Temple, Jerusalem and Passover.

God

In the Bible we see a gradual development in Israel's understanding of who God is. We call this revelation.

Covenant

A covenant is an agreement between two people, between nations or between a powerful person (such as a king) and a weaker people (such as his subjects). Before writing was invented, covenants were oral agreements, usually sealed with a ritual.

Parity covenants are made between equals. Covenants between a powerful person and a weaker people are *vassal covenants*. Moses made a vassal covenant with God at Sinai.

Noah and Abraham had *individual covenants* with God. God promised Noah never again to destroy the world by flood, and Noah agreed to increase and multiply and to eat animals as well as plants. God promised Abraham that his descendants would be as numerous as the stars and possess the land of Israel forever. Abraham promised to be circumcised.

Law

The terms of the covenant are contained in the Ten Commandments, which eventually developed into 631 laws when written down in the

Torah. This was the Law, the code of the covenant.

Circumcision

Circumcision was probably a sign of giving the generative powers back to God. It became a sign of the covenant relationship with God.

Ark of the Covenant

The Ark was the chest in which the Israelites carried the tablets on which the Ten Commandments were inscribed. It was a sign that God was always with them. When the Israelites entered the promised land, they kept the Ark in a sacred shrine at Shiloh.

Shrines

Shrines were special places that were regarded as sacred in ancient times had prohibitions and privileges attached to them. People made pilgrimages to these sacred places, which were serviced by priests. Before entering the shrine, a person had to perform certain rites. One privilege always granted in a holy place was *asylum*, which meant "You are safe here."

Priests

Priests served as interpreters of God's will and offered sacrifice at shrines. Later, after the Temple was built, shrines were no longer used, and the priest's dual role as interpreter and offerer of sacrifice was divided.

Prophets

Prophets became the interpreters of God's word and often served as advisers to kings.

Kings

Regarded as saviors of their people, kings protected them from enemies and saw that the law was carried out.

Priests, prophets and kings were anointed. *Messiah* means "anointed one."

Sacrifice

Sacrifice was the primary act of worship. Often it was a way of atoning for sin, both individual and communal. The Day of

Atonement, Yom Kippur, was an annual day for communal atonement. Israel also offered communion sacrifices and sacrifices of thanksgiving and dedication. (Mary and Joseph offered two doves when dedicating Mary's firstborn to God.) Sacrifice was offered on an altar, which represented God.

Temple

After Solomon built the Temple in Jerusalem, the city acquired great importance. People were required to go to the Temple for the pilgrimage feasts: Passover, Pentecost and Tabernacles.

Sacrifice was offered only in the Temple. Its construction reflected peoples' importance in society: The center, the holy of holies, was God's dwelling place; outside it lay the courtyard of priests, then the courtyard of Israelite men, then the courtyard of women and, finally, the courtyard of Gentiles.

Passover

Passover, the feast of the paschal lamb, was the chief annual feast. Celebrated in spring, it recalled all of the Israelites' history, especially their escape from Egypt, and summed them up as a people.

Your Notes

Review

Buzzwords

See if you can define the following:

God

Covenant

Circumcision

Law

Ark of the Covenant

Shrine

Priest

Prophet

King

Sacrifice

Altar

Temple

Jerusalem

Passover

Summing Up

Take five minutes to sum up below what you have learned.

For Discussion

Your Questions

In the space below, write any questions you have. Share these questions in your small group. After your small group's discussion, report its conclusion to the larger group.

Other Possible
Topics for
Discussion

- The concept of sacred space today

- The Mass as a sacrifice

- Relating the concepts of king, prophet and priest to Jesus

Follow-Up Activities

On Your Own

Read over the outlines and your own notes on this presentation.

We as Christians have a covenant relationship with God. Our half of the agreement is to love one another. List ways in which you can show your love for your family and neighbors. Then do it!

Write below what you learn from these activities.

For Further Reading

Scripture From Scratch:

McBride, Alfred, O. Praem. "David: Israel's Poet King." N0595

_____. "From Mount Sinai to the Sermon on the Mount: The Law of Moses." N1194

Smith, Virginia. "Exodus and Exile: Shaping God's People." N0295

Zannoni, Arthur E. "The Biblical Prophets: Challenging Role Models." N0994

Catholic Update

McBride, Alfred, O. Praem. "The Ten Commandments—Sounds of Love From Sinai." C0989

Map

Plan of the Temple

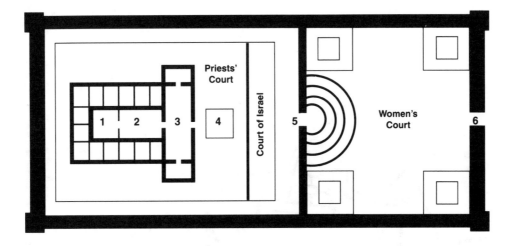

1 Holy of Holies   **4** Altar
2 Holy Place   **5** Nicanor Gate
3 Porch   **6** Beautiful Gate

Map

Jerusalem at the
Time of Jesus

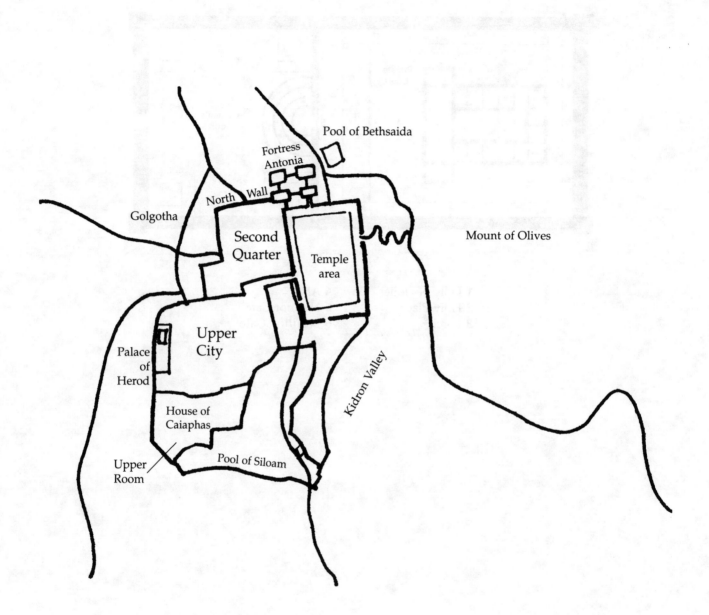

Pool of Bethsaida

Fortress
Antonia

North Wall

Golgotha

Second
Quarter

Temple
area

Mount of Olives

Upper
City

Palace
of
Herod

Kidron Valley

House of
Caiaphas

Upper
Room

Pool of Siloam

PROGRAM THREE

Tracing Our Family Tree: The History of the Hebrew People

Presented by Virginia Smith

Program Outline

Heritage is important. People of all times and places have asked three great questions: Where did we come from? What are we doing here? Where are we going? While God's history stretches from eternity to eternity, biblical history only deals with plus or minus two thousand years in one specific part of the world.

Prehistory

Primeval or primordial history is that period predating written records and preserved for following generations through oral tradition. All ancient societies possess some account of their beginnings (Where did we come from?) in the form of a myth. A myth is not untrue; it is merely nonfactual, usually stating one or more great truths in a fanciful manner, either because data-based material is unknown or unavailable or because no one can provide a firsthand account. The Genesis creation stories (Chapters 1—2) come from this genre, as does most of that book's material through Chapter 11.

Modern exploration of space constantly expands our understanding of our universe and its origins. God has not changed, but our capacity to comprehend creation has. We are growing in our perception.

Pre-Christian Religious History

The Hebrew Scriptures contain religious history. It was usually recorded long after the fact, which tended to influence how it was recorded. Looking back on events often alters their interpretation. These early accounts are historical rather than straight history. Their many authors did not intend to record history in the sense we do today, but rather to record the ongoing story of God and his people.

Because some two thousand years are involved, we'll break that time into more manageable five-hundred-year segments, highlighting only major events.

The Age of the Patriarchs (2000-1500 B.C.E.)

Actual biblical history begins with Abraham, the first seemingly historical character, who probably lived about the mid-nineteenth century B.C.E. He was probably ethnically Semitic and is referred to as Hebrew, a term of uncertain meaning. He was a patriarchal figure, meaning he had a position of authority over a large extended family. A foundational figure for three world religions (Judaism, Christianity and Islam), he did not found any of them. Abraham is called the Father of Faith because he set out on an arduous journey, knowing neither its purpose nor its destination; he believed he would have an heir when there was no reason to believe that; and he was willing to sacrifice that son when asked to do so. In any case, he knows almost nothing about the God he is dealing with and even less about his own role in connection with that God.

In the patriarchal line, Isaac succeeds Abraham, Jacob (Israel) succeeds Isaac, and Jacob's dozen sons form the fourth and last generation of Patriarchs. From them stem the twelve tribes of Israel. One of their number, Joseph, sold into slavery in Egypt by his jealous brothers, becomes instrumental in moving the family to Egypt, where they lived happily after—for a while.

The Age of Moses, Joshua and the Judges (1500-1000 B.C.E.)

Joseph's family remained in Egypt some 430 years. During that time, their lot deteriorated from honored guests to suffering slaves. Enter Moses, a unique Israelite raised with one foot in the Hebrew culture and one in the Egyptian. To him fell the unenviable task of convincing the pharaoh to release his people, then to shepherd those people through the Sinai Desert and into the Promised Land (Canaan). While camped at the foot of Mount Sinai, the Israelites entered into a covenant with God, the heart of which was the Ten Commandments.

The journey to Canaan was long and hard, spanning two generations. The job of elbowing into the already populated Canaan was assigned to Moses' aide and successor, Joshua. After many a skirmish with the local citizenry, Joshua managed to get the Israelites settled and distribute the land among them.

After Joshua, no one stepped into the leadership role. The tribes fended for themselves and were easy prey for their stronger neighbors. Local deliverers known as judges saved the day on many occasions, but after about two hundred years, the Israelites asked the last of the judges, Samuel, for a king. They got one: Saul. His reign began with promise and ended in disaster during the latter half of the tenth century B.C.E. after a long love/hate relationship with the man who would be his successor and Israel's greatest king, David.

The Age of the Monarchs (1000-500 B.C.E.)

With David, we come to the apex of Israel's history, its bright, if brief, moment in the sun. David finally conquered Jerusalem, expanded Israel's borders, brought the Ark of the Covenant to Jerusalem and toyed with the idea of constructing a temple to house it. God elects to build a "house" for David instead, foretelling a dynasty of kings that would endure perpetually.

David was followed by his son, Solomon. Where David extended Israel's borders, Solomon extended them farther. Where David constructed great buildings, Solomon created more and greater ones, including the Temple.

Solomon's heir, Rehoboam, was not cut from the same cloth. So inept was he that the secession of ten tribes ensued almost immediately. The northern tribes retained the national identity: Israel. The southern nation became known as Judah and retained Jerusalem as capital, the Temple as worship center and the Davidic kings as rulers.

In 721 B.C.E., Israel fell to the superpower of the day, Assyria. Much of the populace was deported and never returned, becoming the "ten lost tribes."

Judah survived until 587 B.C.E., when a similar fate befell it at the hands of the Babylonians. Marched into exile, the Judahites spent about half a century in Babylon until released when the Persians came to power. The remnant of those exiled returned to a desolate land and a ruined Jerusalem. It was time to begin again.

The Age of Restoration (500 B.C.E. to Beginning of the Christian Era)

Rebuilding was a long, arduous process for the Judahites (Jews). Nehemiah rallied the demoralized returnees and galvanized them into action—rebuilding the city walls and gates. Zerubbabel led reconstruction of the Temple, although this version was vastly inferior to Solomon's grand structure. Ezra returned from exile carrying the Torah and sank the Jewish community's religious roots deeply into the new era.

The fourth to second centuries B.C.E. saw Alexander the Great and his generals stamp the Hellenistic influence on the eastern Mediterranean. The last of that was dislodged in the second century by the Maccabees, who restored some semblance of self-rule to Judah under the Hasmonean dynasty.

But in 63 B.C.E. a new ascendant power, Rome, captured Jerusalem. Little more than half a century later, a new era would begin, changing Judah and the wider world forever.

Your Notes

Review

Buzzwords

See if you can define the following:

Primeval history

Myth

Oral tradition

Patriarch

Semitic

Exodus

Judge

Decalogue

Exile

Remnant

Restoration

Summing Up

Take five minutes to sum up what you have learned.

For Discussion

Your Questions

In the space below, write any questions you have. Share these questions in your small group. After your small group's discussion, report its conclusions to the larger group.

Other Possible Topics for Discussion

- Ways in which the history of the Israelites served to form them as a people

- Examples of exodus and exile experiences in your own life

- How terms such as *Promised Land*, *Sinai Desert* and *Chosen People* can be used as metaphors

Follow-Up Activities

On Your Own

Spend some time thinking about how your personal history or your family history has formed you as an individual.

For Further Reading

Scripture From Scratch

McBride, Alfred, O. Praem. "David: Israel's Poet King." N0595

McNamer, Elizabeth. "Where Did We Get Our Bible?" N0796

Smith, Virginia. "Abraham: God's Chosen Person." N1096

_____. "Exodus and Exile: Shaping God's People." N0295

Zyromski, Page McKean. "Moses: The Man the Lord Knew Face to Face." N0496

Catholic Update

Zannoni, Arthur. "Jesus the Jew." C1193

A Time Line of Great Events
in Hebrew History

B.C.E. (Before
Common Era)

c. 1850	Abraham travels to Canaan from Ur
c. 1650	Sons of Jacob (Israel) settle in Egypt
c. 1250	Moses leads the Israelites out of Egypt: the Exodus
c. 1200	Israelites settle in Canaan; Joshua distributes the land to the tribes
c. 1000	King David makes Jerusalem the capital of Israel
961-922	King Solomon rules Israel and builds the Temple in Jerusalem
922	King Rehoboam rules; kingdom splits: Israel in north, Judah in south
721	Assyria conquers Israel; "ten lost tribes"
587	Babylon conquers Judah, destroying Jerusalem and beginning the Exile
538	Persia ends the Exile, allowing the Jewish remnant to return home
520-515	Second Temple is built
c. 333	Alexander the Great conquers Jerusalem
323-197	Ptolemies from Egypt rule Palestine
197-142	Seleucids from Syria rule Palestine
164	Revolt of the Maccabees
142-63	Hasmonean dynasty rules an independent Judea
63	Rome conquers Jerusalem
37-4	Herod the Great, King of Judea
c. 7-4	Birth of Jesus

Piecing It Together: What Archaeology Can Tell Us

Presented by Elizabeth McNamer

Program Outline

Until two centuries ago we had no evidence to support what was written in the Bible. Since the development of the science of archaeology, we now know a great deal that we did not know before. Archaeology gives us material evidence of how life was lived.

The Hebrew people were greatly influenced by their neighbors and borrowed extensively from them. Excavations in Mesopotamia show that the Hebrew people acquired many of their ideas from the land "between the rivers." The Hammurabi Law Code predates the Ten Commandments by six hundred years. The creation myth of the Sumerians, *Enuma Elish*, is older than the creation myth in Genesis. The ziggurats in Mesopotamia are connected to the Genesis story of the Tower of Babel. A flood similar to Noah's is found in the *Gilgamesh Epic*. King Sargon and Moses were both found in the bulrushes as babies.

Evidence that Semitic people occupied Egypt in the seventeenth century B.C.E. is found in the tomb painting of Beni Hasan, where people wearing "coats of many colors" are led into Egypt. The Israelites may have been influenced by the Egyptian symbols: the snake, the golden bull and the ark. No archaeological evidence in Egypt supports the Exodus event. It is the interpretation of the events that is important. Neither is there evidence that the walls of Jericho tumbled down in 1200 B.C.E., although Hazor and Gibeon were destroyed at this time. Biblical stories are meant to be theological rather than factual.

What Archaeology Tells Us About...

Canaanites. They were a conglomeration of tribes occupying land that stretched from Egypt to Syria. It seems that they practiced fertility rites and human sacrifice.

The Philistines. They were "sea people" who may have come from Cyprus and invaded Israel at the same time as the Hebrews. They had iron weapons, which made them successful soldiers.

The Kingdom. The first Israelite king was Saul, who lived modestly. Archaeology shows that David, who captured Jerusalem, had a rich life-style. Solomon lived very well with an ample supply of food, wives, concubines, horses and palaces. Solomon built the Temple. After the division of the kingdom, Samaria became the capital of the north. Samaria's King Ahab built himself a palace of ivory, which has been excavated.

The Assyrians. They were warlike tribes in northern Syria who invaded and destroyed the northern kingdom of Israel in 720 B.C.E. They attempted to destroy Jerusalem and laid siege to it. We now can read the other side of the story on King Sennacherib's prism.

The Babylonians. King Nebuchadnezzar, who took over in Babylon, conquered and took the Jews into exile in 586 B.C.E. Babylon was a city of dazzling opulence where the Jews lived quite well. They built synagogues and started writing down their laws and traditions.

The Persians. King Cyrus succeeded the Babylonians and sent the Jews home to Israel. They rebuilt their temple under Ezra and Nehemiah.

The Greeks. The Greeks under Alexander the Great were the next big power on the horizon. The Seleucids took over after Alexander died. They built the city of Antioch in Syria and several other Greek cities. They tried to impose Greek ideas on the Hebrews.

The Romans. The Romans arrived in Israel under General Pompey in 63 B.C.E. They renamed Israel *Palestine* and were there at the time of Jesus. The greatest archaeological find from Roman times is the discovery in 1947 of the Dead Sea Scrolls, written by the Essene community at Qumran between the second century B.C.E. and the first century C.E.

The ordinary person's life. The ordinary person lived in constant fear under the threat of war. The city gates served as the town meeting place where men gathered to talk. (Women talked at the well.) They had their little luxuries; perfume bottles, mascara applicators and golden earrings occasionally turn up at digs. Burial of the dead was important. The corpse was put in a rock-cut tomb immediately after death. Someone went to visit the tomb three days after burial to make sure the person was dead. When flesh deteriorated, bones were put in ossuaries.

Your Notes

Review

Buzzwords

See if you can define the following:

Archaeology

Code of Hammurabi

Mythology

Tomb at Beni Hasan

Gibeon

Canaanites

Philistines

Assyrians

Babylonians

Persians

Greeks

Romans

City gates

Summing Up

Take five minutes to sum up below what you have learned.

For Discussion

Your Questions

In the space below write any questions you have. Share these questions in your small group. After your small group's discussion, share its conclusions with the large group.

Other Possible Topics for Discussion

- Does archaeology enhance the study of the Bible? If not why not? If so, how?

- What is mythology?

Follow-Up Activities

On Your Own

Read over the outlines and your own notes on this presentation.

Reread the creation stories in the first two chapters of Genesis and then write your own creation myth.

Read the story of the Gibeonites in Joshua 9—10.

Read the description of the Ark in Exodus 37 and make a drawing of it.

Write below what you learned from these activities.

For Further Reading

Scripture From Scratch:

McNamer, Elizabeth. "Archaeology at Bethsaida." N0495

Pixner, Bargil, O.S.B. "The Galilee Where Jesus Walked." N0696

The Ancient Near East

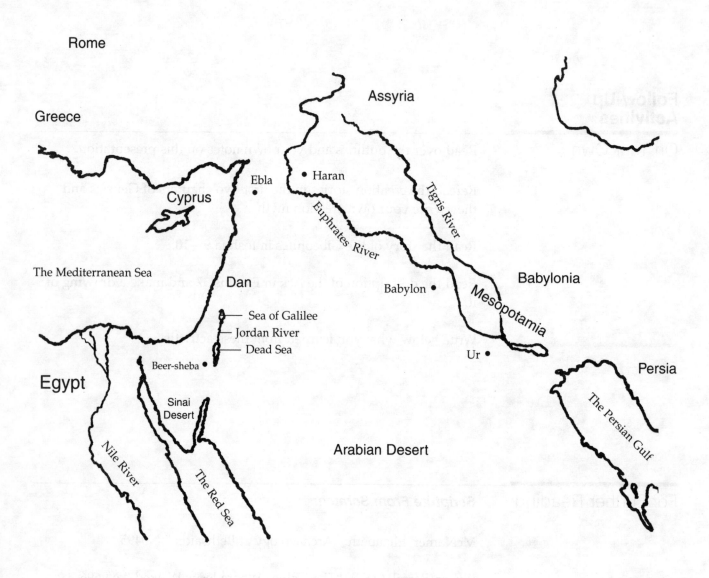

Rome

Greece

Assyria

Ebla

Haran

Cyprus

Euphrates River

Tigris River

The Mediterranean Sea

Dan

Babylon

Babylonia

Mesopotamia

Sea of Galilee

Jordan River

Dead Sea

Ur

Persia

Beer-sheba

The Persian Gulf

Egypt

Sinai
Desert

Nile River

The Red Sea

Arabian Desert

PROGRAM FIVE

People, Places and Feasts: Religious Life in Jesus' Day

Presented by Virginia Smith

Program Outline

The world in which Jesus lived in many respects defined him. It is difficult, if not impossible, to understand Jesus without positioning him within a specific culture and time period.

Many factors characterize a person; among them, nationality, religion, family, occupation, education, age, gender. One of the most crucial in assessing Jesus is simply that Jesus was Jewish. Born into a family of observant Jews (see Luke 2:21-50) and reared in a Jewish culture where both religious and secular affairs were governed by Mosaic law, Jesus was thoroughly Jewish.

People and Places

The Temple

The centerpiece of Jewish life, [illegible]
Jerusalem's Temple Mount fo[illegible]
was destroyed by the Babylon[illegible]
much more modest, but sump[illegible]
Great continued throughout Je[illegible]
C.E., three decades after Jesus' d[illegible]
the Temple at various points in [illegible]

For centuries before Jesus, Jews [illegible]
homeland. Most Mediterranean [illegible]
No matter where they lived, Jew[illegible]
feasible for the three annual pilgr[illegible]assover, the Feast of Weeks (Pentecost) and the Feast of Booths (Tents, Tabernacles). En route, pilgrims sang pilgrimage psalms (Psalms 120—134).

Synagogues

The word *synagogue* means "assembly." Synagogues may have originated during the Babylonian exile (sixth century B.C.E.). Where Temple worship centered on sacrifices, synagogue services centered on prayer and instruction in the Hebrew Scriptures. Even during the period of the second Temple, synagogues continued to be found in every Jewish community. Jesus took part in services (Luke 4:15-30).

Sabbath

From sundown Friday to sundown Saturday, Jews observed the sabbath, as decreed in the Decalogue (Exodus 20:8-11). Jesus was sometimes impatient with the many rules and regulations which surrounded sabbath observance in his time (Mark 2:27) and clashed with the scribes and Pharisees over interpretation.

Scribes and Pharisees

The term *Pharisee* probably meant "separated ones" and identified a Jewish sect centered on strict observance of the Mosaic law. Laymen, the Pharisees were closely allied to the scribes (teachers and interpreters of the Law). Scribes, highly respected scholars and intellectuals, were usually addressed as "rabbi."

Jesus went head to head with these leaders because he felt that they had circumscribed the prescriptions of the Law with so many rules for observance that the original intent was lost. Still, these were deeply religious men, and not all of them opposed Jesus.

Sadducees

This term may mean "righteous" and refers to a Jewish sect largely made up of the priestly aristocracy, conservative landowners and merchants. Sadducees differed from Pharisees on such theological issues as the resurrection of the dead and the existence of angels. Accepting only the Torah as authoritative, Sadducees seem to have had little or no Messianic doctrine. Also at odds with Jesus on more than one occasion, the Sadducees disappeared following the final destruction of the Temple in 70 C.E. The Judaism that survived was Pharisaic and rabbinical.

Priests and Levites

The role of priest, a hereditary office, was to officiate at sacred functions, primarily sacrifices. Priests were initially from the line of Aaron, Moses' brother, and later from the line of Zadok, which might have been somehow connected to Aaron's family.

Levites traced their lineage to Levi, son of Jacob (Israel). They were distinct and separate from the priests and subordinate to them. They performed a number of functions in the Temple, ranging from musicians and maintenance workers to doorkeepers and security police. Priests belonged to the tribe of Levi, but not all Levites were priests.

Essenes

Never mentioned in the Christian Scriptures and largely unknown until the mid-twentieth century, the Essenes introduced themselves to us by way of their library, known today as the Dead Sea Scrolls. Their name possibly identifies them as "the pious ones," and they may have emerged as a group some one hundred fifty years before Jesus. Believing mainline Judaism corrupt, they shunned population centers for their own community of Qumran near the Dead (Salt) Sea and met their end at the hands of the same Roman army that leveled Jerusalem in 70 C.E.

Sanhedrin

This council of seventy-one members constituted the ultimate authority in matters religious during the Roman occupation. Assuring public order was a major priority of this group. Jesus appeared before them following his arrest (see Matthew 26:59-60). Lacking the power to execute (although they were empowered to sentence blasphemers to stoning), the Sanhedrin referred Jesus' case to the Roman procurator, Pontius Pilate.

Feasts and Observances	Rosh Hashanah, the Jewish New Year, ushers in a ten-day period known as the High Holy Days or Days of Awe. Falling during September or October on today's calendar, these days are set aside for repentant Jews to examine their lives, pray for forgiveness and ask a blessing on the coming year. The period closed with Yom Kippur, the Day of Atonement, which calls for, if possible, a total fast from food and drink.

Five days after Yom Kippur, Jews celebrate Sukkot, the Feast of Booths, commemorating the years of nomadic desert existence during the Exodus. In Jesus' time, the feast was also a harvest celebration and was sometimes referred to as the Feast of the Ingathering.

In December, Hanukkah, the Feast of Lights, memorializes Judas

Maccabeus' rededication of the desecrated Temple in 164 B.C.E. Candles are lighted each evening; gifts are exchanged and parties held.

The most loved of Jewish festivals is probably Passover, which tells the ancient story of Israelite homes being passed over during the tenth and final plague, which killed all Egyptian firstborns and precipitated the Exodus. The centerpiece of this observance is the Seder, a ritual meal which the Synoptic writers connect to the Last Supper.

Before Jesus' disciples were called Christians, they were known as followers of the Way, a new way of expressing and living Judaism. Christians owe a great deal to their ancestors in the faith.

Your Notes

Review

Buzzwords

See if you can define the following:

Temple

Synagogue

Sabbath

Scribe

Pharisee

Sadducee

Priest

Levite

Essene

Sanhedrin

Rosh Hashanah

Yom Kippur

Sukkot

Hanukkah

Passover

Summing Up

Take five minutes to sum up what you have learned.

For Discussion

Your Questions

In the space below, write any questions you have. Share these questions in your small group. After your small group's discussion, report its conclusions to the larger group.

Other Possible
Topics for
Discussion

- The role of religion in forming the identity of a people

- Whether it was Jesus' intent to form a new religion, Christianity, or to fulfill the existing religion, Judaism

- How and why Matthew's Gospel especially stresses the Jewishness of Jesus

- The sad history of anti-Semitism in Christianity

Follow-Up Activities

On Your Own

Look for evidence of improved Jewish-Christian relations.

Plan a visit to a synagogue or other Jewish center.

Read works by Martin Buber and other modern Jewish thinkers.

For Further Reading

Catholic Update:

Guinan, Michael, O.F.M. "The Creation Story of Genesis: Does It Really Contradict Evolution?" C0694

Zannoni, Arthur E. "Jesus the Jew." C1193

Under the Roman Boot: The Political Situation in First-Century Palestine

Presented by Elizabeth McNamer

Program Outline

We know about this period in history from Roman historians: Josephus, who was a Jewish historian; Philo of Alexandria (another Jewish writer); the Dead Sea Scrolls and the Gospels.

After Alexander the Great, Israel came under the jurisdiction of the Greek governor of Syria. The Greeks tried to impose their ways, their religion and customs, on the Jews. The Jews rebelled against Greek rule under the Maccabees, who became known as the Hasmoneans and set themselves up as kings and priests. John Hyrcanus ordered all in Galilee to become Jews at the turn of the first century B.C.E., when many Jews returned from Babylon.

Enter Rome

There was much infighting among the Hasmoneans. In 63 B.C.E. one of them asked for Roman help in ousting his younger brother, who had made himself both high priest and king. Rome dispatched General Pompey. Once the Romans were there, they stayed. Now Jewish rulers were mere puppets of Rome and Israel was a province in the Roman Empire. Israel was renamed Palestine. Herod was appointed king by the Romans in 37 B.C.E.

The Roman Empire was vast, extending from the Atlantic to Syria. The Romans had a genius for government. They divided the Empire into provinces and appointed able men as governors. Roman soldiers built roads, all of which led to Rome. Rome collected taxes from one wealthy person, who then collected from everyone else.

Rome named Herod the Great king in 37 B.C.E. Josephus does not record that Herod ordered the killings of any babies in Bethlehem, but the crime was certainly in character. Herod had a great building program. He built several cities, including Caesarea and Sebaste. He built a mountain in the desert and called it Herodium. He had several sumptuous palaces, including three on Masada.

When Herod died, his territory was divided among his three surviving sons. Herod Antipas became Tetrarch of Galilee. Philip Herod became Tetrarch of Gaulinitis. Archelaus received Judea and Samaria and title of Tetrarch. He was so cruel that the Jews requested he be replaced with a Roman procurator. The fifth procurator was Pontius Pilate.

Agrippa I, the grandson of Herod the Great, became king of the land of his grandfather. His son, King Agrippa II, succeeded him.

Zealots

Zealots believed that the Messiah would be a military leader. Scholars debate when they came into existence.

Messianic Expectations

The Essenes expected the Messiah to be a high priest or a prophet. Rome had a constant headache in dealing with messiahs, particularly at festival times, when Jerusalem was crowded with pilgrims. Romans despised the Jews but allowed the Sanhedrin to rule and pass judgment on religious laws.

Crime and Punishment

Jews could stone people for disobeying religious laws. Crucifixion required a crime against Rome. Jesus was tried on political charges and judged by Pontius Pilate, whom Josephus describes as mean-spirited and cruel, with no regard for Jewish law. Philo of Alexandria says that Pilate liked to vex the multitude, was a man of inflexible disposition, merciless as well as obstinate.

Jesus entered Jerusalem riding a donkey, as did the early Hebrew kings. He was tried before Pilate on charges of claiming to be king. The sign over his cross, written in Latin, Greek and Hebrew, read "Jesus of Nazareth, King of the Jews."

Your Notes

Review

Buzzwords

See if you can define the following:

Maccabees

Herod the Great

Caesarea

Archelaus

Herod Antipas

Philip Herod

Zealots

Essenes

Sanhedrin

Summing Up

Take five minutes to sum up below what you have learned.

For Discussion

Your Questions

In the space below, write any questions you have. Share these questions in your small group. After your small group's discussion, report its conclusions to the larger group.

Other Possible Topics for Discussion

- Archaeology shows that Herod the Great had a grand life-style, while that of Jesus was simple. Discuss how we are influenced today by the life-styles of the rich and famous.

- In Mark's Gospel, Jesus often seems to reject the title *Messiah*. How do you relate this to the fact that the Zealots were expecting a Messiah who would be a military leader?

Follow-Up Activities

On Your Own

Read over the outlines and your own notes on this presentation. Look up in a map the extent of the Roman Empire.

Israel at the time of Jesus was living under a foreign power. Write how you might feel if you were living under foreign domination.

For Further Reading

Scripture From Scratch:

McNamer, Elizabeth. "King of the Jews: The Herod Dynasty." N1295

Zannoni, Arthur E. "'Who Do People Say That I Am?'" N1095

Time Line

Rulers of Palestine

Greeks (Seleucids)   320-175 B.C.E.

Maccabees (Hasmoneans)   175-63 B.C.E.

Romans   63 B.C.E.-70 C.E.

Roman Emperors

Augustus   34 B.C.E.-13 C.E.

Tiberius   14-36 C.E.

Herod Family

Herod the Great   37-4 B.C.E.

Herod Archelaus   4 B.C.E.-6 C.E.

Herod Antipas   4 B.C.E.-39 C.E.

Philip Herod   4 B.C.E.-34 C.E.

Herod Agrippa I   37-44 C.E.

Herod Agrippa II   50-c. 100 C.E.

Bed, Bread and Business: Daily Life in First-Century Judea

Presented by Virginia Smith

Session Outline

History usually records earth-shaking events and larger-than-life figures, but in any age most people are caught up in the more mundane happenings of their own day-to-day lives.

Jesus may be a universal savior, but he was very much a product of his own time and place. Models for his parables were drawn from the everyday images around him, images which are often foreign to us today. These can often be clarified by reconstructing the everyday lives of Jesus' contemporaries.

Meeting Basic Needs

Food

Barley bread was a staple of the poor. Barley or lentil soup was also common. Rural areas had better access to fresh produce, although many fruits and vegetables were marketed in cities such as Jerusalem. Butchers could be found there as well, serving a moneyed clientele. (The poor rarely ate meat.)

Most families ate two meals a day, a light breakfast and a substantial dinner. Cooking was done outdoors in good weather, indoors in bad. Aside from bread, hot foods were generally boiled in a pot, served in a common bowl and eaten with fingers or using bread as a utensil.

Life was different for the wealthy. Banquets were common and food was served on expensive plates. Fine wine flowed freely and fancy imported foods were commonplace. Jesus often attended such feasts; he compared the Kingdom of God to them (Matthew 8:11 and 22:1-14).

Wine was the usual drink with meals. Bread and wine were certainly the most universal examples of sustenance in Jesus' day.

Clothing

As in many parts of the world, cloth was made at home by spinning and weaving. Galilee produced fine linen from flax grown locally, but the wool trade centered in Jerusalem. Jesus' basic tunic would have been homespun. Over it, he would have worn a loose-fitting mantle with fringes, bound by a leather belt or cloth girdle. A cloth might have been placed on his head and allowed to hang to his shoulders.

Women wore much the same type of tunic as men, but their mantles were fuller and were often tucked up to form a kind of apron. Both genders wore sandals of palm bark or wood with leather straps.

Housing

City families lived in one- or two-room cubes of whitewashed, oven-dried brick with dirt floors. Roofs were flat and doors were narrow. People slept on mats, covered by their mantles. Houses were often bunched around courtyards, where women did cooking and laundry. Some courtyards had cisterns for water storage.

Country villagers lived similarly. If their houses were two-level, people lived in the upper level and domesticated animals below. Habitable caves abounded, and both people and animals have lived in them from ancient times to modern.

Wealthy families frequently lived in limestone mansions with open courtyards, pools, gardens, baths with hot running water—even central heat.

Health Care

Disease was thought to be the result of sin and its punishment; it implied a disrupted relationship with God. The Parable of the Good Samaritan (Luke 10:30-37) is a graphic description of the treatment of injuries. Saliva was thought to have healing power (Mark 7:33; 8:23). Physicians were not among the admired trades. Bronze surgical instruments dating from Jesus' time have been found near Jerusalem. Midwives delivered babies. As is still true today, the type of health care depended to some extent on the patient's ability to pay.

Education

A small-town boy like Jesus began formal schooling at age five, usually at the local synagogue. All learning was done from the Torah. At about ten, he would advance to broader subject matter, learning to apply the principles of the Torah to daily life. Gifted students might go on to study under scribes (doctors of the law). Formal education usually ended at about age 18.

Rabbis at the Temple in Jerusalem had schools of disciples for advanced study. Paul was sent from his home in Tarsus for such an education (see Acts 22:3).

Formal schooling was usually not available for girls. Their mothers were their teachers, providing instruction in how to observe the dietary laws, how to raise their children properly, how to treat routine illnesses and injuries.

Travel

Tourists were few; travel was expensive, difficult, dangerous and uncomfortable. Capricious weather, roadside bandits, wild animals and shipwreck were only some of the hazards. Travelers tried to reach the relative safety of cities before their gates were closed and barred for the night. Offering hospitality to strangers was more than courteous; it was essential. Often, travelers attached themselves to caravans or other groups.

Hostelries were few and unpredictable. While some were quite elaborate, most were rudimentary, tending more to the safety of animals than to their owners.

Although Israel was not a maritime nation for most of its history, by Jesus' day Herod's thriving port city, Caesarea, hosted ships from many nations and made export trade possible.

Your Notes

Review

Buzzwords

See if you can define the following:

Flax

Mantle

Doctor of the Law

Caravansary

Summing Up

Take five minutes to sum up what you have learned.

For Discussion

Your Questions

In the space below, write any questions you have. Share these questions in your small group. After your small group's discussion, report its conclusions to the larger group.

Other Possible
Topics for
Discussion

- Whether daily life in Jesus' day would have been more or less stressful than our own

- Whether people's priorities have changed much or little from that time to this

- How we might go about simplifying our lives and/or reordering our priorities

Follow-Up Activities

On Your Own

Attend a local celebration of heritage where such arts as spinning, weaving and grinding are demonstrated. Watch the skill involved. Think how different your time commitments would be if you had to factor tasks like these into your schedule.

For Further Reading

Scripture From Scratch:

Zannoni, Arthur E. "Biblical Prophets: Challenging Role Models." N0994

_____. "'Who Do People Say That I Am?'" N1095

Catholic Update:

Zannoni, Arthur E. "Jesus As Prophet." C1294

Carpenter, Rabbi, Messiah: Jesus in His Own Times

Presented by Elizabeth McNamer

Program Outline

Sources

The sources for the life of Jesus are the Gospels, Josephus, the Torah, Philo of Alexandria, the Dead Sea scrolls, archaeology and early traditions of the Church. The historical Jesus is the person of flesh who walked, talked, taught and interacted with others and observed the customs and rituals prevalent in first-century Palestine before the Resurrection.

According to the Gospels, Jesus was born in Bethlehem. He lived in Nazareth in Galilee, which had been a place of Gentiles since the Assyrian conquest of 734. During the reign of John Hyrcanus (104-103), many Jews were encouraged to return from Babylon (perhaps the ancestors of Jesus were among them) and all inhabitants were ordered to become Jews (by circumcision) or to leave the country.

Inhabited from the beginning of the first century B.C.E., Nazareth was a village of about a hundred people. Nazoreans were "of the shoot of Jesse" and were therefore of the family of David. Nazareth means "village of the shoot."

Mark's Gospel says that Jesus had brothers—James, Joseph, Judas and Simon; tradition has it that he had three sisters. These were possibly children of Joseph by an earlier marriage. The Temple Scroll of the Dead Sea Scrolls tells that it was not uncommon for a woman who had taken vows of virginity to marry a man, take care of his household and still have her vows respected. Joseph was a carpenter, a *technon*—one who works with stone, a master builder; Jesus probably worked with him. As a builder, Jesus may have worked at Sepphoris, a Greek town being built some three miles from Nazareth. If so, Jesus may have known Greek.

An old tradition says that Anna, the mother of Mary, had a sister, Elizabeth, who lived in a town in Judea. This would make John the Baptist and Jesus cousins.

Rabbis (teachers) did not begin their career until the age of thirty. When John was baptizing in the Jordan river near Jericho, Jesus spent some time with him. Jesus returned to Nazareth and proclaimed to his family and tribe who he was. They thought he was crazy. He moved to Capernaum and called disciples.

Capernaum was an important fishing town. Fishing was the major industry in Galilee of the time. Fishermen were middle-class businessmen and were probably bilingual if not trilingual. Politically, Capernaum was a little more tenuous. It lay in the domain of Herod Antipas, whose behavior was unpredictable. Gamla, a Zealot town, was ten miles away.

Religion

As far as religion was concerned, there were three Torah schools. The *Sadducees* were the priestly aristocracy. The *Essenes*, also priestly but disapproving of Temple worship, had a few monastic centers, the most famous of which is Qumran. They were mostly celibate but had many adherents who were married. They had a community at Mount Zion and other groups scattered around the country, including one at Bethany. The Essenes had their own calendar and always celebrated Passover on Wednesday. The *Pharisees*, the "separate ones," were great observers of the Law and surrounded the laws with other regulations in order to safeguard it. All three groups accepted the Torah but interpreted it differently.

Jesus belonged to none of them. He had his own *halaka* (interpretation of the Law). Many people felt constricted by the law. Jesus' mission was to free.

Reign of God

There was a common belief that the reign of God was about to begin. The Zealots interpreted this as meaning that Israel would have autonomy and that the Messiah would be a military leader. The Essenes saw it as God intervening in history and they saw the Messiah as being either a priest or a prophet.

Jesus preached that the reign of God was within and that it encompassed all nations. His teachings on the Kingdom were usually accompanied by miracles. Most of his miracles were performed around the evangelical triangle of Capernaum, Chorazim and Bethsaida.

He visited Gentile territory. Many Jewish sects did not approve of associating with Gentiles. The woman with the hemorrhage was probably a wealthy Gentile, according to Eusebius. Jesus' extending of the reign of God to Gentiles released his followers from the Jewish laws.

Jesus ventured into Gentile territory when he went to Caesarea Philippi. This was "Camp David" for the Romans as well as for Herod Philip. The gates to Hades were there. There Jesus said to Peter, "You are Peter and upon this rock I will build my church." The Transfiguration probably took place here on Mount Hermon.

Jerusalem

Jesusalem, dominated by the Temple, was about eighty miles away. The Synoptic Gospels suggest that Jesus went to Jerusalem for just one Passover. John's Gospel suggests that he went there for three. Jesus probably stayed at Bethany.

The Gospels give conflicting accounts about the celebration of the Passover. John insists that Jesus was crucified on the eve, when the lambs were being slaughtered in the Temple. Jesus could have celebrated the Passover on Wednesday, when the Essenes were celebrating it. They let out rooms at a monastic community at Mount Zion for guests to have the feast.

The Jewish authorities could have killed Jesus by stoning. They wanted him crucified by the Romans because that would condemn his message as well. One who hung on a tree was accursed.

This was done. It was supposed to be the end of him. It was only the beginning of his message. And that message has changed the world.

Your Notes

Review

Buzzwords

See if you can define the following:

Historical Jesus

Netzer

Rabbi

Technon

Capernaum

Halaka

Torah schools

Caesarea Philippi

Summing Up

Take five minutes to sum up below what you have learned.

For Discussion

Your Questions

In the space below, write any questions you have. Share these questions in your small group. After your small group's discussion, report its conclusions to the larger group.

Other Possible Topics for Discussion

• What types of people did Jesus associate with?

• How political was he?

• What was his relationship with his family? With John the Baptist?

• What do you think Jesus was trying to accomplish?

Follow-Up Activities

On Your Own

Read over the outlines and your own notes on this presentation.

Look up all the towns associated with Jesus on a map of Galilee. How long would it have taken him to go from one place to another? See if you can find any pictures of Galilee.

Read the account of the wedding feast at Cana (John 2:1-11). Put yourself in the scene. What if any conversation do you think took place between Jesus' family and his disciples?

Write below what you have learned from these activities.

For Further Reading

Scripture From Scratch:

Pixner, Bargil, O.S.B. "The Galilee Jesus Walked." N0696

Reid, Barbara, O.P. "It's a Miracle: Signs and Wonders in Scripture." N0995

Zannoni, Arthur E. "'Who Do People Say That I Am?'" N1095

Catholic Update:

Langenbrunner, Norman. "The Psalms: Prayers That Lead Into the Living God." C0387

Senior, Donald, C.P. "Jesus the Physician: What the Gospels Say About Healing." C1290

Map

Map of Galilee

Sidon •

Tyre •

Mediterranean Sea

Galilee

Caesarea Philippi •

Jordan River

Chorazim •

Capernaum • • Bethsaida

Cana •

Magdala • Sea of Galilee

Gamla •

Kursi •

Tiberias •

Hippos •

Sepphoris •

Nazareth •

Jordan River

Beth-shean •

Appendix

For Facilitators: How to Use *Scripture From Scratch II*

In order to use *Scripture From Scratch II* effectively, it's important to know what it is and what it isn't, who is likely to benefit most from it and how best to set it up.

What *Scripture From Scratch* Is and Isn't

Scripture From Scratch is *not* a comprehensive Bible study program, an ongoing process which more or less systematically examines individual books, groups of books or themes in some detail. That was not the purpose for which it was created. Programs of that kind are certainly on the market, targeted for Catholic adults; some are excellent.

Scripture From Scratch, far from being designed to compete with such programs, should in most cases *precede* them. *Scripture From Scratch* is like the overture to the opera or ballet or Broadway musical (choose one to fit your tastes). In an overture the primary themes surface, but they are generally touched on only briefly. Full development comes later in the score.

Also, parish pews contain a good many potential Bible students who have built-in resistance to anything that seems like a class where they're going to look silly. It was primarily for these folks that *Scripture From Scratch* was fashioned.

In the process of getting people over that initial hurdle that distances them from formal study, *Scripture From Scratch* attempts to do (and *not* do) several things:

   to put participants thoroughly at ease (not to terrify anybody);

   to share our own enthusiasm for God's word (the Bible is *not* boring);

   to present a solid introduction to the Bible (not to waste people's time);

   to keep the mood light and friendly (not to remind people of the class they disliked most in school);

to leave participants feeling they want more—and more and more!

If the last effort is successful and people do leave *Scripture From Scratch* with a hunger for even meatier contact with the Bible, then the stage is set for one of those ongoing programs. The earlier apprehension will be past and a new and totally justifiable confidence will have taken its place. People will realize that whatever deficiencies in biblical background they may have had were not grounded in personal shortcomings and, better yet, that the Bible can be tackled with assurance, with success and with enthusiasm.

As facilitator, you would do well to keep in mind that there should be plans in the works for study programs to follow *Scripture From Scratch*. To bring people to a heightened level of interest and simply leave them there can result in tangible frustration, even anger. *Scripture From Scratch* is not the be-all and end-all. *Scripture From Scratch* is square one.

Who Will Benefit Most?

This question has already been answered from one perspective. Initially, the target audience was seen as adult Catholics with little or no Bible background who lacked enough self-confidence to participate in whatever opportunities their parishes provided. That there are sizable numbers of persons who fit that description is attested to by the multitudes who have been *Scripture From Scratch* participants thus far. That this is not a local phenomenon is attested to by the fact that these have usually been the majority group wherever these sessions were presented. In urban or rural settings, Western states or Eastern, the situation proved very nearly uniform.

Reaching this segment of Catholic congregations should remain *Scripture From Scratch*'s basic function, but by no means its only one. Others may benefit just as much.

As a facilitator, don't overestimate those individuals who *do* have some experience with the Bible. The content of a *Scripture From Scratch* session is more than adequate to challenge them to new perceptions of previously acquired knowledge and a grasp of totally new ideas. Furthermore, those who already have some exposure to biblical lore often encourage newcomers, who see in them a glimpse of themselves later on.

Everyone engaged in catechetical or liturgical ministry will profit from participation in these sessions. Because so much of today's catechetical material is biblically based, *Scripture From Scratch* can provide excellent groundwork for volunteers or professionals teaching on any level from preschool to adult. This is especially true if the texts they use are lectionary-based.

The lectionary leads us quite naturally to the lector, that person whose ministry is to proclaim the word of God to the People of God. The key word here is *proclaim*. Although frequently referred to as "readers," lectors are intended to be a good deal more than that. The sense of the passage should almost spring from the lector's lips with clarity and conviction. That's a tall order when the lector is uncertain of the biblical writer's intention or misreads it. The better the lector knows the Bible, the better (and more effective) the proclamation.

What age groups seem most attracted to *Scripture From Scratch*? Generally speaking, those between 17 and 100. That may appear a bit facetious, but the truth is that, while teens don't usually arrive in large numbers, they do arrive. But this is not a youth-oriented program and probably would not be well suited to a high-school religion class or a parish religious education program.

Older folks are something else again. It is both surprising and edifying to see how many of them participate. Often they are among the most ardent listeners in the room. They don't miss much, and they love to ask questions. These wonderful people are often the catalysts who energize everyone else and set the wheels of discussion in motion.

In between the very youngest adults and the very oldest you'll find the rest of the grown-up population of your parish. Every one of them is a candidate for *Scripture From Scratch*, and a good mix of ages, sexes, educational and occupational backgrounds quite often produces the best group interaction. In a nutshell, then, any Catholic who fits into the adult category will probably fit into *Scripture From Scratch*.

Grown-Ups Aren't Kids

One of the most important things you, as facilitator, need to keep in mind is that you are not dealing with children; you are working with adults, and the learning process is decidedly different.

Children as a rule come to a topic—any topic—as so many blank slates waiting to be written upon. The instructor, therefore, pretty much has carte blanche in the construction of course outlines or laying out the building blocks of learning.

Adults, on the other hand, arrive with well-worn slates which have been written on again and again. Some of what was written has long since been erased. Some has been rubbed out and figured over. Some small amount is indelible and remains no matter what, and that's called life experience. Every adult arrives at a new experience dragging all that life-experience baggage along behind. Not one of us can abandon it or even turn in our old slates for new ones untouched by human experience. Mostly we wouldn't want to, but the point is that every new piece of information is filtered through what is already known, what has already happened, what is (correctly or incorrectly) perceived and mindsets and thought patterns which are fairly solidly in place. It's not that adults have their minds firmly nailed shut and don't want anything to disturb the status quo. On the contrary, most of those who attend *Scripture From Scratch* will be there because they're eager to learn. It's just that this is an entirely different process from what you may be accustomed to if your previous experience has primarily been with children.

This should not make you uncomfortable or in the least apprehensive. Quite the opposite; it's exciting because you can expect to learn every bit as much from the participants as they learn through the material you make available to them. It's decidedly a two-way street, and this makes for some fascinating discussions. Since no two people's life experience has been the same, no two outlooks will be, either.

Not too many years ago, it was unusual to see adults involved in the formal learning process. While lifelong learning was a fact, it was generally done in the well-known school of hard knocks or the college of experience, not in an academic setting. Change began after World War II ended. Hundreds of thousands of American servicemen and women came marching home and marched straight into college classrooms, which greeted them with open arms (if classrooms can be said to have such appendages). Supported by the GI Bill, these older students took their places next to the younger students and quickly became fixtures in schools across America.

Another postwar development was the arrival of high technology, which set economic institutions on their collective ear much the way the Industrial Revolution had done centuries before. As machines took over jobs formerly held by humans, the humans were forced to rethink and retrain. Many started entirely new careers at or past the midpoint of their lives.

Once we were into this new world of minute-to-minute change, change so rapid it was described as future shock, it became evident that everybody would have to scramble to keep up or be left behind. So, whatever the field, ongoing study became a necessity rather than an interesting option. It was said that a bachelor's degree in engineering was good for a mere eight years if nothing was done in the meantime to stay abreast of developments in the field.

College classrooms now contain large numbers of students in their 30's, 40's, 50's and beyond. "Beyond" belongs to new ideas like Elderhostel, a learning process for retired folks whereby they can visit campuses almost anywhere in America for a week or two in the summertime and enjoy all manner of subjects taught by college faculty.

So if Catholic educators go with the flow, they should fully expect to find large numbers of parishioners of all ages who are no strangers to the concept of lifelong learning. And, if there's any field in which that idea should find a home, it's in the area of faith development. As God's people grow older, they should become increasingly aware of the need to know God better in order to love God more and serve God with greater dedication. There's *always* more to be done in faith expansion.

Treat Your Grown-Ups Like Grown-Ups

Keeping in mind what was previously said about the staggering numbers of adults in the learning pool, you'll want to adjust your facilitating style accordingly. Among other things, this will mean using a collaborative approach. Your principal duty will be to create an environment which facilitates learning or, as was said earlier, to make things less difficult. An adult is a full partner in the learning process, not a child to be lectured to or talked at for prolonged periods. Thus, the more active participation you can promote, the better.

In summary, the best adult learning experiences are achieved in an atmosphere which:

1) is centered on the adult learner rather than the instructor or facilitator;

2) can be plugged into the individual's own life: past, present, future;

3) is open to the direction each individual wants or needs to take it (no "homework" but lots of suggestions on ways to implement material);

4) is practical (adults live in the real world and want everything to relate to that).

Your role as facilitator is not so much to stand out as to fit in, not so much to be the ranking authority on any and all topics but to be the member of the group who makes it easier to work with the material.

There now, don't you feel better?

Large Group or Small?

How large a gathering should you plan for? That may depend on several factors, not the least of which is the size of your television screen. If you have access to a large-screen TV (forty to forty-eight inches) and if your facility is correspondingly large, you may elect to invite the entire parish or even neighboring parishes for a one-afternoon session utilizing one of the *Scripture From Scratch* programs. That's often a great way to get your parish program under way. And actually, that's the way the original *Scripture From Scratch* was designed to be presented and the way we usually do it in person.

Still, one of the program's strong points is its versatility. There are any number of ways it can be done. If you prefer the more conventional once-a-week approach, you may easily stretch one unit across four weeks. Or add a second unit for an eight-week period. One such eight-week schedule in the fall could be followed by another eight weeks of *Scripture From Scratch II* in the winter or spring, thereby presenting the entire package in a single year. Eight weeks is workable for most people, but many hesitate to commit themselves to more than that.

Programs such as RENEW are built around small-group meetings. The small-group setting may be more suitable for you, especially if your parish already has such groups in place. Videotapes can be very effective in living rooms because a comfortable atmosphere ordinarily prevails. Each group should have its own facilitator, so it might be wise to hold a get-together for prospective leaders ahead of time.

Of course, small groups can also meet in parish surroundings. If the TV screen is small, that may well be the better option. When people have to strain to see or hear, they rapidly lose interest.

Parishes are not the only logical settings for these presentations. Retreat houses, renewal centers and educational institutions often have outstanding facilities and attract participants from a wide area.

Creating the Atmosphere

In times past, it was usually thought that adequate preparation had been made for a group project if the room had four walls plus floor and ceiling, a working light bulb and a rack of the obligatory hard-backed folding chairs. (After all, a little penance is good for the soul—even if it does little or nothing for the spine.)

Today, thankfully, another school of thought prevails when it comes to environment. Perhaps all our concern about the earth's environment has spilled over to interior settings. Whatever the reason, adults expect—and are entitled to—more than a bare-bones setting. Again, remember that working with adults is quite different from working with children or teens. Many adults arrive for evening sessions after putting in a full day on the job. They're tired. They want and need some place to deposit their weary bones, and those folding chairs are not the answer.

If at all possible, provide seating that offers a clear view of the TV screen and you, the facilitator—seating which is, above all, comfortable. Realistically, you may not have many options in your parish, but certain other Christian denominations excel in their attention to such amenities. It isn't uncommon to visit a Protestant church which has a warm and cheerful room devoted to adult gatherings, a room that is fully carpeted and furnished with upholstered chairs and sofas, handy tables and table lamps. Unless your parish is somewhat avant garde, you may have to make do with less luxurious surroundings. As that wonderful old saying goes, do the best you can.

Atmosphere serves another important purpose. First impressions are vital, and the first impression participants will get of this or any other program is the setting in which it will be presented. At all costs, avoid anything remotely resembling a classroom. Even if your participants are not openly spooked by such a setting, they will not find in it anything warm or welcoming—which is, above all, the way you want to be perceived. This allays the fears of those who arrive with some trepidation and increases their confidence that they will, indeed, survive.

Americans tend to presume that if coffee is being served, the situation can't be all bad. That may not appear in any psychology book, but it definitely appears in the subconscious of a good many people. Therefore, consider providing coffee, tea and a cold drink of some kind. It seems to be easier to socialize over a cup, so make beverages available as soon as participants arrive, allowing them a few minutes to mix and mingle before the session begins. This idea is especially significant before the opening session, when introductions probably need to be made. Informal, personal introductions are far less intimidating than going around the room and asking each individual to reel off his or her name (although logistics often make this exercise necessary as well).

Each presentation of *Scripture From Scratch* is full to the brim with content, much of which will be new to a majority of those present.

Although time for group discussion is provided in the program format, informal discussion over refreshments is just as essential. For that reason, it is strongly recommended that a break be provided following each session, especially if you have programmed two or more presentations for a single day. A substantial amount of meat is presented in each talk, and time will be needed to chew, swallow and digest it. Generally speaking, that will be done in three distinct ways: interaction with the entire group, one-to-one conversations during the breaks and personal meditation later in the day, the week, the month or the year. All of these are necessary inasmuch as information remains little more than facts and figures until it is assimilated, meshed with life's prior experience and made part of a total faith outlook.

Additional Resources

Another way to make data one's own is to write out those thoughts which seemed particularly striking or which might not be remembered if left to chance. This study guide provides ample space for note-taking. For that reason (and a number of others) every person participating should be provided with a copy. It will prove extremely useful during the sessions and even more so thereafter when it will fill the need for a continuing reference.

Although the material presented in the various units of *Scripture From Scratch* is designed to accommodate the needs of a wide variety of Catholic adults, it should be readily acknowledged that particular communities, areas or groups often have particular needs. Some topics require more investigation than an overview is equipped to provide. Frequently, situations of this type can be addressed by making one or two additional resources available. A list of these is provided in the bibliography at the back of this guide. As facilitator, you may elect to order an inexpensive resource, such as issues of *Catholic Update* or *Scripture From Scratch*, in quantity.

Which Translation of the Bible?

One question that is almost sure to arise early is: What Bible do I use? In times past, that wasn't even a consideration. The first Catholic-authorized Bible in the English language was, ironically, named for two French cities and thus dubbed the Douay-Rheims translation. It met the needs of Catholic refugees from England after Henry VIII's difference of opinion with the papal authority on the matter of divorce. The New Testament of this version was published at Rheims in 1582, and the Old Testament at Douay at 1609. Ultimately, both were revised in the mid-18th century by Bishop Richard Challoner. From that time until the mid-20th century, the Douay-Rheims remained the Catholic English translation, while the King James version held a comparable position in the Protestant world.

During the first half of the 20th century, the American Bishops' Committee on the Confraternity of Christian Doctrine (CCD) was commissioned to produce a more modern English translation of the traditional Vulgate, the Latin text originated in the early fifth century by St. Jerome. With the promulgation of *Divino afflante Spiritu* by Pope Pius XII in 1943, those plans were abruptly changed as emphasis was shifted to a return to the original biblical languages. This trend has produced a host of new translations, some of which have already undergone revision (see page 77).

(The frequency with which biblical translations are revised is a good indication of how much we are learning and how rapidly we are learning it. Occasionally you may be asked when we will finally have a single English translation of the Bible which will endure. The answer is never. In dealing with the living word of God, it is impossible to exhaust it—or to say that any one translation is *the* definitive one which will never need to be changed, updated or even modernized as to language style.)

The New American Bible With the Revised New Testament and the Revised Psalms, Confraternity of Christian Doctrine, 1991. The NAB is the translation most often heard in liturgy in the United States. Highly readable and with adequate introductions, notes and cross-references, it was first introduced in 1970. Its New Testament was revised in 1986 to reflect advances in scholarship and to attempt more inclusive language; a new translation of Psalms was added in 1991. Editions ranging from paperback New Testaments to leather-bound, gilt-edged editions are available from several publishers; prices range accordingly.

The New Jerusalem Bible, general ed. Henry Wansbrough. Garden City, N.Y.: Doubleday and Company, Inc., 1985. Since it first appeared in English in 1966, The *Jerusalem Bible* has achieved a reputation for offering an extremely readable text along with some of the finest introductions and notes for the individual books of the Bible. This revised edition offers all the features for which the original *Jerusalem Bible* was respected plus the newest advances in such areas as theology, linguistics and archaeology. Additionally, it attempts more inclusive language.

A translation that has been enthusiastically received by many Catholic, Protestant and Orthodox communities is the *New Revised Standard Version*. Published in 1990, the *NRSV* was written for the majority of English-speaking readers rather than for academics. As a result, it has been praised for its clarity of thought and ease of expression. Other attributes include its use of inclusive language and incorporation of all writings seen as sacred by any branch of Christianity.

One translation that is popular with many Catholics is *Today's English Version*, possibly better known as the *Good News Bible*. Published by the American Bible Society, an interdenominational organization, the *Good News Bible* is available in either cloth or paperback editions which contain the deuterocanonical books (apocrypha), which often do not appear in Protestant editions of the Old Testament.

The greatest advantage of the *Good News Bible* can sometimes also be its greatest drawback: its ease of reading. Because this translation was created for those for whom English is a second language or those whose reading skills are limited, translators were specifically confined to a strictly circumscribed vocabulary that can become repetitious and simplistic, although the basic intention of words and passages is extremely clear.

Yet another edition which may well show up in the hands of your participants is the *Living Bible*. What is not always understood even by those who use this version is that it is not a translation at all, but rather a paraphrase. While a translation attempts to turn an existing text into another language with as much accuracy as possible (given that no language translates perfectly into any other), a paraphrase restates the sense of the passage in the author's own words, thereby leaving a sizable amount of room for personal interpretation. This may make for interesting comparisons on the part of advanced biblical students but may be troublesome for the beginner. A reliable translation such as those listed above is usually a better choice.

Now and then, someone will arrive with a Douay-Rheims. The best thing to say about that is to say nothing at all. If the person is comfortable with that version and has used it a long time, fine. As time passes, the advisability of moving to a more modern translation usually becomes evident, and the person makes the switch. In fact, it's helpful to own two or three translations to compare difficult passages or to utilize diverse sets of notes.

Over and above all other considerations is the goal of having all participants come to a point where they regard the Bible as "user-friendly." Finding their way around with ease and confidence can do a lot toward turning Bible skeptics into Bible students.

Bibliography

Bibles

It is frequently beneficial to have two or more biblical translations on hand in order to compare them for clarity of thought and the particular insights their reference materials provide. When selecting a Bible, check the title page to determine whether the version is indeed a translation of the text from the original languages or is only a paraphrase which provides the general sense of the text as interpreted by an editor. A good modern translation is always to be preferred to a paraphrase. (See page 75 for recommended translations.)

The Catholic Study Bible, general ed. Donald Senior, C.P. New York: Oxford University Press, Inc., 1990. In addition to the notes and introductions included in any *New American Bible* edition, this unique volume features background articles on every biblical book by some of America's finest Scripture scholars. Written in an extremely readable style, these articles are accompanied by a set of fourteen indexed maps and by other helpful writings on such topics as biblical history and geography, archaeology, how the Bible fits into Catholic life and its use in the lectionary.

The New Oxford Annotated Bible with the Apocryphal/Deuterocanonical Books, general ed. Bruce M. Metzger and Roland E. Murphy. New York: Oxford University Press, Inc., 1991. This New Revised Standard Version has been well received for the clarity and accuracy of its thought and expression. It also attempts to eliminate gender-biased vocabulary and to incorporate all sacred writings used by any branch of Christianity: Catholic, Orthodox or Protestant.

Reference Materials

Bergant, Dianne, S.S.A., and Robert J. Karris, O.F.M., eds. *The Collegeville Bible Commentary*. Collegeville, Minn.: The Liturgical Press, 1989. One of the most widely used biblical commentaries in American Catholic circles today, the Collegeville series was originally published as a series of booklets (twenty-five for the Old Testament, eleven for the New) which have now been gathered into a single volume. The individual booklets are also still available. The single volume contains no Scripture text, while the booklets include the New American Bible text. Because some of America's foremost names in Catholic biblical studies are to be found among the authors, the Collegeville Commentary provides excellent resources in a most readable style.

Brown, Raymond E., S.S., Joseph A. Fitzmyer, S.J., and Roland E. Murphy, O. Carm., eds. *The New Jerome Bible Handbook*. Collegeville, Minn.: The Liturgical Press, 1992. As its title implies, this is a greatly condensed version of its parent, *The New Jerome Biblical Commentary*. A simplified introduction to every biblical book and highlights from each are provided along with digests of *NJBC* topical or general articles. A world of sound biblical scholarship is packed in delightfully readable fashion between the covers of this unique publication.

_____. *The New Jerome Biblical Commentary*. Englewood Cliffs, N.J.: Prentice Hall, Inc., 1990. Even though the prestigious *NJBC* may be beyond the average Bible student in both its cost and its highly scholarly approach, no listing of Catholic reference works on the Bible would be complete without it. First published in 1968, the *NJBC* has now been totally updated (two-thirds of the material contained in it is new). This statement alone should provide insight into how rapidly the world of Scripture study moves and changes and why the Bible is so often described as the living word of God.

Frank, Thomas Harry, ed. *Atlas of the Bible Lands*. Maplewood, N.J.: Hammond, Inc., 1984. Due to the unfamiliarity of many place names in the Bible and also because many of these names changed (sometimes several times) during nearly two thousand years of history, a biblical atlas is a must. The minimal maps provided at the back of most Bibles are rarely adequate to such a mammoth task. This compact ser of maps provides in an economy of pages and price a tremendous aid in settling locales firmly in people's minds.

Kodell, Jerome, O.S.B. *The Catholic Bible Study Handbook: A Popular Introduction to Studying Scripture*. Ann Arbor, Mich.: Servant Publications, 1985. In one small volume which slips easily into a book bag alongside the Bible, Father Kodell has assembled a wealth of valuable information to guide the novice (or one who has been at it awhile) into the wonderful world of the Bible. This compact paperback would make an excellent foundational study for a person or a group just launching into the word of God.

Kohlenberger, John R., III., ed. *The Concise Concordance to the New Revised Standard Version*. New York: Oxford University Press, 1993. Slim in size, this valuable reference nonetheless contains some sixty thousand biblical references under nearly eight thousand headings plus short biographies of some three hundred biblical figures and six hundred commonly used biblical phrases.

Matthews, Victor. *Manners and Customs in the Bible*. Peabody, Mass.: Hendrickson Publications, 1991.

May, Herbert G., ed. *Oxford Bible Atlas*. New York: Oxford University Press, 1984. A somewhat more comprehensive work than Hammond's, the *Oxford Bible Atlas* contains a substantial amount of explanatory text in addition to an outstanding set of biblical maps. Many of these maps appear at the back of *The Catholic Study Bible* from the same publisher.

Mazar, Amihai. *Archaeology of the Land of the Bible*. New York: Doubleday, 1990. Long and detailed, primarily for the serious student of archaeology, though others will also enjoy it.

McKenzie, John L., S.J. *Dictionary of the Bible*. New York: Macmillan Publishing Company, 1965. Although somewhat older than most recommended reference works, McKenzie's work has become a standard and is most useful in the same way secular dictionaries are. It defines and explains terms, names, places, ideas, themes and concepts which appear in the pages of the Bible and which may often be bewildering without a good guide.

Murphy-O'Connor, Jerome. *The Holy Land: An Archaeological Guide from Earliest Times to 1700*. New York: Oxford University Press, 1996. Father Murphy-O'Connor, who teaches New Testament at the Ecole Biblique in Jerusalem, takes us on a tour of the Holy Land and its archaeological sites. Great companion for a trip.

VanderKam, James. *The Dead Sea Scrolls Today*. Grand Rapids, Mich.: Wm. B. Eerdmans Publishing Co., 1994.

Periodicals

The Bible Today. The Liturgical Press, Collegeville, MN 56321. Well respected both for the quality of its writings and the caliber of its writers, this bimonthly is somewhat challenging in content. Many of the renowned names in Catholic biblical studies are regular contributors, yet their articles are intended for a general audience.

Biblical Archaeology Review. P.O. Box 10757, Des Moines, IA 50340. Geared toward Bible-lovers who have a special interest in the science of archaeology, this nondenominational bimonthly attempts to steer a strictly scientific course. It does not use its findings to prove the Bible right or wrong on particular points. Often it provides more questions than answers. Although some of its advertising is highly sectarian, the articles themselves are frequently illuminating.

God's Word Today: A Daily Guide to Reading Scripture. P.O. Box 7705, Ann Arbor, MI 48107. A monthly magazine, *God's Word Today* focuses each issue on a particular scriptural book or theme. A suggested reading is provided for every day of the month, followed by a short commentary, a question or two for reflection and a short prayer. Several longer articles devoted for the most part to the same topic give additional background. *God's Word Today* is sound scholarship on a popular level.

Scripture From Scratch, St. Anthony Messenger Press, 1615 Republic Street, Cincinnati, OH 45210. A monthly publication, edited by *Scripture From Scratch* video presenters, Elizabeth McNamer and Virginia Smith, each issue contains a meaty article by popular authors well qualified in writing about the Bible plus discussion questions, prayers and suggestions for applying the word of God to everyday life. Ideal for Bible study groups or individuals, *Scripture From Scratch* in print can also be used in conjunction with the *Scripture From Scratch* videos.

Topical Reading

The Catholic Approach to Scripture

Brown, Raymond E., S.S. *The Critical Meaning of the Bible.* Mahwah, N.J.: Paulist Press, 1981.

_____. *Responses to 101 Questions on the Bible.* Mahwah, N.J.: Paulist Press, 1990.

Catechism of the Catholic Church, Libreria Editrice Vaticana, United States Catholic Conference, Inc., 1994, Part One, Section One, Chapter Two.

Dogmatic Constitution on Divine Revelation, Vatican Council II: The Conciliar and Post Conciliar Documents, Austin Flannery, O.P., gen. ed. Northport, N.Y.: Costello Publishing Company, 1987.

Harrington, Daniel, S.J. *Interpreting the New Testament.* Collegeville, Minn.: Liturgical Press/Michael Glazier Press, 1979.

_____. *Interpreting the Old Testament*. Collegeville, Minn.: Liturgical Press/Michael Glazier Press, 1979.

Murray, Daniel A. *The Living Word in the Living Church: A Guide to What Every Catholic Should Know About Scripture, Tradition and the Teaching Office*. Nashville, Tenn.: Catholic Bible Press, 1986.

Ralph, Margaret Nutting. *And God Said What?* Mahwah, N.J.: Paulist Press, 1986. An accurate and extremely readable treatment of that element of the historical-critical approach to biblical studies known as form criticism. Introduces the reader to such literary forms as myth, gospel and apocalyptic writing as they are used in various biblical books.

St. Romain, Philip. *Catholics' Answers to Fundamentalists' Questions*. Liguori, Mo.: Liguori Publications, 1984.

Old Testament

Auer, James, and Robert Delany, S.T.D. *The Bible: A Simple Introduction*. Los Angeles: Franciscan Communications, 1988.

Benware, Paul N. *Survey of the Old Testament*. Chicago: Moody Bible Institute, 1988.

Boadt, Lawrence, C.S.P. *Reading the Old Testament: An Introduction*. Mahwah, N.J.: Paulist Press, 1984.

Charpentier, Etienne. *How to Read the Old Testament*. New York: The Crossroad Publishing Company, 1982.

Kramer, William, C.PP.S. *Evolution and Creation: A Catholic Understanding*. Huntington, Ind.: Our Sunday Visitor, 1986.

Link, Mark, S.J. *The Psalms for Today*. Valencia, Calif.: Tabor Publishing, 1989.

Martin, George. *Reading Scripture as the Word of God: Practical Approaches and Attitudes*. Ann Arbor, Mich.: Servant Publications, 1982.

Matthews, Victor. *Manners and Customs in the Bible*. Peabody, Mass.: Hendrickson Publications, 1991.

McBride, Alfred, O. Praem. *The Ten Commandments: Sounds of Love From Sinai*. Cincinnati, Ohio: St. Anthony Messenger Press, 1990. The commandments are often perceived as a list of "don'ts." This author sketches them in a more positive light as "values for loving."

Rohr, Richard, O.F.M., and Joseph Martos. *The Great Themes of Scripture: Old Testament.* Cincinnati, Ohio: St. Anthony Messenger Press, 1987. By treating themes the authors help their readers grasp the big picture, including the development of major ideas over the centuries.

Shanks, Hershel. *Ancient Israel.* Washington, D.C.: Biblical Archaeology Society, 1988. Excellent reference if you want to know about the people who wrote the Old Testament by the editor of *Biblical Archaeology Review.*

Stuhlmueller, Carroll, C.P. *New Paths Through the Old Testament.* Mahwah, N.J.: Paulist Press, 1989.

New Testament

Arav, R. and J.J. Rousseau. *Jesus and His World.* Minneapolis: Fortress Press, 1995. This informative book discusses all the archaeological sites in Israel and their connection to Jesus and his ministry.

Brown, Raymond E., S.S. *An Introduction to New Testament Christology.* Mahwah, N.J.: Paulist Press, 1994. Although Brown is one of America's most respected Scripture scholars, he possesses the uncommon talent of being able to write on a popular level as well. This volume introduces the reader to Jesus, the Christ, on a number of different levels and from a number of different perspectives. An excellent foundation for those who don't know Jesus and for those who think they do.

_____. *A Coming Christ in Advent.* Collegeville, Minn.: The Liturgical Press, 1988.

_____. *A Crucified Christ in Holy Week.* Collegeville, Minn.: The Liturgical Press, 1986.

_____. *A Once and Coming Spirit at Pentecost.* Collegeville, Minn.: The Liturgical Press, 1994.

_____. *A Risen Christ in Eastertime.* Collegeville, Minn.: The Liturgical Press, 1991.

_____. *An Adult Christ at Christmas.* Collegeville, Minn.: The Liturgical Press, 1977.

Freyne, Sean. *Galilee*. Notre Dame, Ind.: Notre Dame Press, 1980. Written by a leading Irish scholar, this is the definitive study of Galilee as it was in the time of Jesus. Somewhat scholarly but quite readable.

Johnson, Luke. *The Real Jesus*. San Francisco: HarperSanFrancisco, 1995. For all who are confused by what they are reading about the Jesus Seminar, Dr. Johnson points out the flaws in the methods used by these scholars and presents the case for the believing Christian.

Marty, William H. *Surveying the New Testament*. Dubuque, Ia.: Kendall-Hunt Publishing Co., 1987.

Matthews, Victor. *Manners and Customs in the Bible*. Peabody, Mass.: Hendrickson Publishers, Inc., 1991. Tidbits about life in biblical times.

McBride, Alfred, O. Praem. *Images of Jesus: Ten Invitations to Intimacy*. Cincinnati, Ohio: St. Anthony Messenger Press, 1993. The various faces of Jesus presented by the Gospel writers.

Meier, John. *A Marginal Jew: Rethinking the Historical Jesus* (Volumes 1 and 2). New York: Doubleday, 1995. A magnificently researched book by a leading Catholic scholar. Heavy reading, but worth it.

Murphy-O'Connor, Jerome. *The Holy Land: An Archaeological Guide from Earliest Times to 1700*. New York: Oxford University Press, 1992. Father Murphy-O'Connor who teaches New Testament at the Ecole Biblique in Jerusalem takes us on a tour of the holy land and its archaeological sites. Great to take with you if you are planning a trip.

Perkins, Pheme. *Reading the New Testament: An Introduction*, 2nd ed. Mahwah, N.J.: Paulist Press, 1988.

Pixner, Bargil. *With Jesus through Galilee*. Collegeville, Minn.: The Liturgical Press, 1993. Written by a Benedictine monk who has spent thirty years walking every inch that Jesus walked, this most enlightening book on the historical Jesus will make Jesus come alive for you. Magnificent pictures of Galilee throughout.

Vanderkam, James. *The Dead Sea Scrolls Today*. Grand Rapids, Mich.: Wm. B. Eerdmans Publishing Co., 1994. Will help you understand what the Dead Sea Scrolls are all about. What you need to know to confute those who have bought into the odd stories circulating about the Essenes, their writings and their connection with Christian origins.

Wijngaards, John. *I Have No Favorites*. Mahwah, N.J.: Paulist Press, 1992. In these books, Wijngaards puts Jesus in context. The reader becomes familiar with Jesus' world in terms of geography, language, social strata and much more.

_____. *My Galilee, My People*. Mahwah, N.J.: Paulist Press, 1990.

Videotapes

Jesus and His Times. Pleasantville, N.Y.: Reader's Digest Home Entertainment Division, 1991. In three one-hour presentations, Jesus' story is told against the backdrop of the time, the place and the culture in which he lived and preached. Superbly produced, these tapes will rivet viewers of all ages.

New Testament: An Introduction. Elizabeth McNamer. Springfield, Va.: The Teaching Company, 1993. A good introduction to the New Testament by one of the Scripture From Scratch presenters. Also available in audio.

Seeking Jesus in His Own Land. Cincinnati, Ohio: St. Anthony Messenger Press/Franciscan Communications, 1987. Stephen Doyle, O.F.M., takes viewers on a "scriptural pilgrimage." Scenes are shot in sites crucial to Jesus' life and public ministry.

ScripturefromScratch

A popular guide to understanding the Bible

edited by Elizabeth McNamer and Virginia Smith

A monthly publication for adults who want to know more about the Bible from the publisher of *Catholic Update* and *St. Anthony Messenger*.

Each monthly, four-page issue contains a meaty 2,000-word article on one topic about the Bible such as the Gospels; the structure, history and development of the Bible; key biblical figures; Christology; background information on geography and archaeology; dogmas and doctrines such as the Resurrection; questions of morality and ethics from a scriptural perspective; and many more.

In addition to a main article every issue includes practical helps to explore the month's article in greater depth:

Praying With Scripture offers ideas for prayer that rlate to the main article.

Talking About Scripture gives questions for reflection.

Living the Scriptures suggests activities to apply the Scriptures to life.

Reading About Scripture includes resources for continued study.

Scripture From Scratch can be used for parishwide distribution, in the classroom, in a small-group setting or for personal at-home study.

Scripture From Scratch Subscription Information

A single subscription is only $11.00 for 12 monthly issues. Bulk rates (copies sent to the same address) are:

2-9: $6.50 each annual subscription
10-99: $3.00 each annual subscription
100-199: $2.40 each annual subscription
200-299: $1.80 each annual subscription
300-499: $1.44 each annual subscription
500-999: $1.20 each annual subscription
1,000 or more: 96› each annual subscription

Example: Get 100 copies per month for one year for only $20.00 a month (100 x 20 cents). Monthly billing available for 50 copies or more to same address.

ORDER FORM

Please send me _____ copies of *Scripture From Scratch* each month for 12 months.

_____ I have ordered a subscription of 50 or more copies. Bill me monthly.

Ship and bill to:

Institution (if applicable) _____

Name _____

Address _____

City/State/Zip _____

Send no money now. We will invoice you for your subscription.

Mail: Tear out this page and mail to St. Anthony Messenger Press, 1615 Republic St., Cincinnati, OH 45210.
Phone: Call toll-free 1-800-488-0488, ext. 158, between 8 a.m. and 5 p.m., EST, Monday through Friday.
FAX: 1-513-241-1197

St. Anthony Messenger Press Guarantee

If you are not completely satisfied with *Scripture From Scratch*, you may cancel at any time and receive a refund for all remaining issues.

CALL TOLL-FREE: 1-800-488-0488